MAN IN A GREY SUIT

Glenn Orgias was raised on the Central Coast of New South Wales. He currently lives in Sydney with his wife, Lisa, and their daughter, Bronte.

Hope you enjoy!

MAN IN A GREY SUIT

GLENN ORGIAS

VIKING
an imprint of
PENGUIN BOOKS

VIKING

Published by the Penguin Group
Penguin Group (Australia)
250 Camberwell Road, Camberwell, Victoria 3124, Australia
(a division of Pearson Australia Group Pty Ltd)
Penguin Group (USA) Inc.
375 Hudson Street, New York, New York 10014, USA
Penguin Group (Canada)
90 Eglinton Avenue East, Suite 700, Toronto, Canada ON M4P 2Y3
(a division of Pearson Penguin Canada Inc.)
Penguin Books Ltd
80 Strand, London WC2R 0RL, England
Penguin Ireland
25 St Stephen's Green, Dublin 2, Ireland
(a division of Penguin Books Ltd)
Penguin Books India Pvt Ltd
11 Community Centre, Panchsheel Park, New Delhi – 110 017, India
Penguin Group (NZ)
67 Apollo Drive, Rosedale, North Shore 0632, New Zealand
(a division of Pearson New Zealand Ltd)
Penguin Books (South Africa) (Pty) Ltd
24 Sturdee Avenue, Rosebank, Johannesburg 2196, South Africa

Penguin Books Ltd, Registered Offices: 80 Strand, London WC2R 0RL, England

First published by Penguin Group (Australia), 2012

1 3 5 7 9 10 8 6 4 2

Text copyright © Glenn Orgias, 2012

Please note: some names, not many, have been changed in order to protect individual privacy.

Design by Adam Laszczuk © Penguin Group (Australia)
Cover photograph © Eugene Tan / Aquabumps
Typeset in Adobe Garamond 12/16pt
Printed and bound in Australia by McPherson's Printing Group, Maryborough, Victoria

National Library of Australia
Cataloguing-in-Publication data:

Man in a grey suit / Glenn Orgias.
9780670076055 (pbk.)
Orgias, Glenn.
Surfers—Australia—Biography.
Shark attacks—New South Wales—Anecdotes.

797.32092

penguin.com.au

FOR LISA

It was too late for surfing, really. But it was beautiful in the water, I remember that. It was dusk, the clouds were purple over the buildings at Bondi, and there is no better place than the ocean to watch the sun set. Light faded and the water turned to ink. It was eerie and magical and quiet, with only the wind and water moving. Sand churned up to the surface after big waves. The chop and spray from the onshore wind slapped my face. I remember that.

The waves were big, wonky and kind of ugly. But it was the best it had been in weeks, and there were thirty other surfers out and paddling onto the junky sets and hassling for the inside position. I don't remember how many waves I caught, maybe three. I can't remember if they were good waves. I would usually remember that, but general anaesthetic has blunted my memory of that time. I would usually remember what turns I did, whether I fell off, what I could have done better, why can the other guy do it, and why the hell can't I?

I caught a wave and paddled back out. I was just inside the crowd when I ducked a small wave and it left white water boiling around me. A lump of swell came from the north, rearing as it approached the sand bank. I changed direction and paddled.

I didn't see it.

It came from behind, and below.

My left arm was shoulder-deep in the ocean. I was pulled backwards by something. In that first instant, I thought another surfer had grabbed me and was trying to stop me catching my wave. I wrenched my arm away. Something massive, much more powerful than me, pulled me under. It shook me with an impersonal aggression.

Before I had a chance to see what it was, before I could really understand what was going on, it was gone. I came up and pulled myself onto my board. I remember the blood – red blood washing over my white board. My arm was in the water, it didn't hurt, and I had a last moment when I was still me.

I pulled my left arm out of the dark water and it all became real. My arm was ripped apart. It looked as though it had been pushed through a circular saw. I was meat. Not good meat. Sinuous meat with yellow bits and bone shards and grey mush: I didn't know so many different-coloured things would be in there. There was a bone jutting out, the skin hanging open, a spiral wound from elbow to wrist. I had gone from whole to empty and it was irreversible.

My hand is off.

Hanging by an inch of skin, my hand was almost amputated.

The shore was 80 metres away. I thought about my wife, Lisa.

I'll never see her again.

She was four months pregnant with our first child.

I looked to shore.

I had everything to live for.

I screamed, and I tried to scream what I had realised, and that scream came out in such a rush, and so much from the gut, that I can hear it now and it doesn't make any sense to me.

'SHARK!'

DAY MINUS 6500

I grew up near the water – in Terrigal, on the Central Coast of New South Wales. It was my dad who taught me how to swim in the ocean, how to duck under breaking waves and swim out deep, and he was the first one to put me on a surfboard. He got me dreaming. When I was a kid I'd pester him to drive me to the beach, and my parents would load up the Toyota with kids, towels, flippers, every manner of boogie board, and my thick blue foam surfboard that was 5 feet long and had a single black rubber fin. I caught my first real wave on that foamie while wearing navy speedos.

When I caught that first unbroken wave and angled across its face, the board racing and moving easily under my feet, I realised that surfing was about speed and weight. The thrill was in the power of the wave breaking, the quickness of the moments flashing by, the shape of the wave, so close and forming its sections, the changing colour of the ocean, the sound, and no second chances, and no time to think.

Dad taught me the basics of surfing, and then Luke showed me what it was to *be* a surfer. I met Luke on my first day of high school. He had a tan running from his fingers to an inch below his short-sleeved shirt, where it had been halted by a wetsuit. He sat next to me at the first rollcall. I put my head down and waited for the teacher to call my name.

'Glenn Orgy-arse.'

That started everyone laughing. I cringed. From under my eyebrows I saw Luke grin and make a what-can-you-do gesture with his hands, and he whispered, 'That was fucked, mate.'

At recess, a conversation started in a circle that I stood on the edge of – the surfers talking about surfing.

'It was 6 foot,' said one kid.

They always said 6 foot, because 6 foot meant it was big and good, and if it wasn't 6 foot it was shit.

'What's the biggest you've surfed?' they asked Luke.

He shrugged. 'About 8.'

Everyone was satisfied with this. I nodded sagely. When the discussion broke up, Luke turned to me.

'You surf on the weekend?' he asked.

'Yeah.'

'Any good?'

The surf had been small.

'6 foot,' I said.

'*6* foot?' He looked amused.

I stuck my chin out.

'Yep.'

While Luke was immediately popular at school, I polarised crowds into friends and enemies. Luke was tanned (massive points), modest and confident, and I wasn't. I was competitive, small and self-aggrandising. I got punched and put in headlocks a lot.

Luke was the best surfer at school – he could do carving turns and spin his board 360 degrees. I was one of the least impressive surfers. But Luke and I were the only ones who lived near Shelly Beach, and so we often surfed together. And when I'd see Luke catch waves I'd scowl at the horizon and will myself to be as good as him. He was at ease in the ocean, while I found it switched moods on me quickly, alternating between serene and treacherous. Sometimes I felt at peace out there, and then in the next moment the ocean trampled me without even noticing I was there. It had a sense of humour, but also a ferocity. There were times when my surfing flowed and I got it right, and those were moments that I lived for. But the ocean could also be a prick of a place. Rough chop. Howling onshore winds. Murky shadows. Weed wrapping around my legrope, rips, set after set of white water, paddling until my arms burned and my spirit faded. Sometimes I wondered why I surfed. Then Luke would do an aerial in front of me and the frustration of it twisted in my chest. He became my best friend, but I envied him too.

Surfing with Luke, I came to know the words 'out there!'

They haunted me. They were code for: 'Paddle. *Paddle!*'

The panic moment was cresting a small wave and seeing a monster behind it.

'Out there!'

To me it meant: 'Get moving. Now!'

Scramble time. Scramble for the hills.

The pack of surfers would flip onto their stomachs, and some were fast enough to crest the wave and go over the back of it, but I was left to paddle towards a wall of ocean, its lip feathering. I raced the wave to the point where its lip would spear into flat ocean and I tried to get under the lip before it broke. I was tempted to let my board go, to push it across the drawing sea and dive below the turbulence. Tempted, but I wouldn't. Letting go was gutless. I'd get shouted out of the water. Getting hammered was better. When the lip landed, I attempted to duck dive. It was only a pantomime, and under the loud rumble of the wave I was a clown attempting to hold a board to his chest. The board would explode away. I'd somersault backwards, and flail until the sea let go and I could come up in the sun, retrieve my board, and spit one word:

'Fuckenhell.'

Having been washed inshore, I'd then paddle back out, infuriated. Luke would say, 'Mate, you got pounded.'

'I know.'

'Why didn't you duck dive?'

'I *did*.'

'*That* was not a duck dive.'

'What was it?'

'I dunno, but it was fucken funny.'

After I learnt to duck dive and to do turns, I realised that the frustration of surfing was part of its appeal. Learning to surf was the culmination of a lot of hard work, and pivotal moments of breakthrough were intensely satisfying. I learnt a lot about surfing from Luke. Not about how to surf, but about having confidence in the water. He was the first real friend I ever had. He was a quiet kid, but we used to laugh and laugh. And push each other. That's just being mates. He shouted me on to bigger waves: '*Yew*. Fucken go!'

And I'd paddle for the bigger ones, because he'd go if it was him. And if I got pounded it wouldn't feel as bad as pulling back from the lip because I didn't have the guts. I never wanted to admit to fear, and, truthfully, I felt like a better surfer than I was when he was watching. The shouts of his encouragement were pearls that I kept secretly. Damn, I wanted to be a good surfer so badly. I kept that secret, too.

Sometimes I wondered if it was my friendship with Luke that led to me surfing or if surfing had led to our friendship. I wasn't sure, but it was a question that stayed with me. Either way, Luke was my best friend for a long time, until things went to shit.

My life came to revolve around surfing at the Point near Bateau Bay with Luke – chaining up my bike at the top of the cliff, unstrapping my board, running down the hill in my wetsuit, across the sand, onto the rock platform. I knew which rocks would be slippery and which ones were sharp with barnacles and limpets. I knew the rocks to wait on, the ones to hop across quickly, and the ones to clamber up to watch the swell steam in and crash. There was a flat rock where I'd put on my legrope. There was a last rock before the land turned into ocean; I'd seen people get washed off there by waist-high water that dragged them backwards, their legs in the air, their boards banging on the rocks. I'd wait while the waves surged over the Point, with the white water swamping my legs. When the surge subsided, I bolted, my legrope in hand, then made skittering steps across the last rock's slippery surface and leapt into the sea, into its heaving foam. I'd sit up with the cliffs of the national park behind me and below them a line of sand running north in an arc before the spinifex.

Out there.

Here: watch the swell come. Watch it rise and gather. It slows as it feels the rock floor beneath and morphs from a thick lump into a steep wall. The good waves develop a bowl-shaped peak. I paddle to the middle of the peak, and spin to face the shore, and feel the wave lift me up its face, and when it is about to pitch, I stand. A sharp drop; the front of the surfboard hanging in midair, my arms above my head, my legs straight. That moment of weightlessness when the back end might slide out, and the fins lose their bite, and the board spins out beneath me, and the lip of the wave drills me into sea. But the board lands flat on the wave face and the fins hold, my knees bend, and I lean over my right shoulder into a turn. Hearing the wave breaking, seeing the wall rise, my back foot pushing on the tail of the board and spraying out a fan of water is the best feeling in surfing for me.

I remember the Point on windless, empty afternoons, when

I stayed out late until street lamps came on and stars appeared, and the waves looked as black as tar and the only difference between the sky and sea was the rippling of the water. I sat at the Point in those dusky moments, my board barely moving, the sea a sheet of glass, white water racing neon to the beach. Those were moments when my mind was perfectly quiet.

Then: catching a wave and arriving on the shore, unstrapping my legrope, wading through the shallows, my arms burning, my legs heavy, my back tight; feeling warm water running out of my wetsuit, exhausted; trudging up the sand, exhausted; stripping my wetsuit off, exhausted. Sitting on the bench with Luke in his backyard and pulling on my sneakers.

'Shit. I have to ride home.'

'Pfft. That would suck.'

Then: riding my bike home on winter nights in tracksuit pants, the surfboard behind me, on a rack, like a sail. Up the last hill and into a warm shower and spaghetti bolognaise and an instant, deep, untroubled sleep.

That was my youth.

When I turned sixteen in February 1991, my family went on holiday to Bali. Luke came too. A guy called Jawbone, a friend of ours, an older local surfer, had given us the rundown on Bali. Jawbone directed us to a bar in Kuta. He told us the code.

'This is it, right: all the hotels over there have pools; if a chick asks you to go for a swim in the pool, that means you're in.'

Luke and I snuck out late and found that bar, and had no problems ordering Bintang beers. The dance floor was heaving. I was young enough to dance without inhibition, and I started dancing with an Australian woman who was much older than me and totally blind. We retired to the bar for a drink and had a conversation that

I cannot remember – apart from her asking me if I wanted to go for a swim in her pool.

'That'd be good,' I said.

She heard a song that she liked and ran back to the dance floor. I told Luke, 'Some chick just asked me to go for a swim.'

'Mate, you're *in*!'

We drank more Bintang. 'December 1963 (Oh, What a Night)' played. We lapped the bar at an increasing pace until the room spun and the night raced away. And then, later, I sat watching the dance floor, having lost Luke to some dark recess until he showed up again.

'Mate, where's that chick?'

'Over there,' I said.

'Which one?'

I pointed.

'The one that's getting onto that bloke?'

'Yeah.'

'Doesn't look like you'll be going for a swim then.'

'Nah.'

I don't remember leaving the bar. I remember heading through the streets of Kuta with the Balinese awake in the early morning, squatting on the dusty roads smoking and watching us stumble along.

Luke and I wanted to surf at Uluwatu, a legendary left-hand break on the south-west of the Bukit Peninsula, which faces into uninterrupted swell travelling north from Antarctic storms. We walked through the jungle to the edge of a cliff, and below was the Indian Ocean. There were only a few surfers in the water; many others were watching from the cliff. The waves looked big. Luke said they were 10 foot. I said 12. It didn't matter. The numbers were only a measure of fear. I said a big number, because when the waves reared up they sounded like jet planes and I knew they were just the biggest fucking waves I'd ever considered surfing. Tim, my fourteen-year-old brother, was with us. I felt that a yawning gap had opened up between my sixteen-year-old semi-adulthood and his fourteen-year-old innocence; I had a vision of him under those big white-water rolls and I told him that he'd have to wait on the cliff.

Luke and I descended the cliff into a cave. The waves washed against the rocks. We didn't speak. We paddled around the waves as they thumped down. Out deep was a diagonal line of surfers waiting on a shifty peak. I sat well outside that crowd, watching, while Luke paddled closer in. Waves shot past me, their lips pitching into the ocean, and I had to scramble over them, hoping each time there wasn't a bigger one behind.

Luke caught a wave. I made half-hearted attempts at waves and got frustrated. I was tentative, I knew it. I was trying to get through it, that tentative uselessness, but it was building and not abating, and it became self-perpetuating. I paddled for waves with lips that barrelled towards me, and pulled back at the last minute when the wall steepened and I saw the shimmer of reef below the surface. I cursed and slapped the water.

Go, you fucken dog.

An inside wave came, well above my head. The first of an arriving set. I paddled hard and caught it. The drop was steep. I stood up with my front foot too far back. I shuffled my foot forward, but lost all speed. I turned up the face of the wave and then turned again just under the lip, trying to stay in front of it, but it hit me in the middle. I smacked against the flat ocean and the air leaving my chest made a sharp sound in its escape.

I sank and was lifted and thrown over the falls with the wave and its spearing lip. When I started fighting the turbulence, I realised I was breathless, and the absence of my breath gripped my throat. The wave dragged me and held me under.

When I came up, I whooped air. The light on the water was blinding. I took a breath before a huge wave crashed in front of me and I dove below its white water. My legrope tugged hard and snapped.

I came up in the wash, my board halfway between me and the cliff. Everything looked huge – the waves, the distance to shore – and my board was just a flip of white in the sea. I felt I was being ripped towards the rocks. I swam. I didn't want to be swimming. I raced a wave that I knew was coming. I stopped to look up and find my board, and I wasn't any closer, because it was moving as fast as I was, or I wasn't moving at all. I thought to yell for help, but the shame of it stopped me. I swam hard.

I sensed a wave behind me. Luke was on it. I waved frantically.

'My board!' I yelled.

Luke cruised past, cutting back, staying with the wave, and further on he kicked off the wave and paddled over to my board. He towed it out into deeper water, away from the waves. I swam to him.

'Thanks,' I panted.

'You alright, mate?'

'Yeah.'

I lay on my board, letting my forehead rest on the deck. It didn't seem so bad now that I was on the board. But I didn't want to paddle out again. Not with those waves beyond any power I'd been in before, with me floating, without my legrope. And I didn't want to have to tell Luke that I wasn't good enough to go out there again.

'Let's go in,' he said.

'Yeah.'

We paddled in and waded back through the cave. My legrope had broken at the swivel. We trudged up the cliff and didn't say much. Tim was waiting, as bored as shit, and hot, and he didn't say much either. I showed him my busted legrope and we watched sets of waves roll in and surfers weaving across their blue faces, and it just looked so easy from up there.

When the adrenaline died down, I was disappointed. I had lost, had been humiliated. Beaten by the waves, and the surfers, and the guys on the cliff, and by timidness, and by Luke. And I was angry.

On the flight home from Bali, we sat in bulkhead seats right up close to a wall onto which movies were projected. I had already seen the movies, but watched them again because they were only inches from my face. I closed my eyes to get away from the kaleidoscopic pixels, and I thought that I was lucky to have a mate like Luke. I admired him. He'd stick by me.

He never made a big deal about that day at Uluwatu. We hadn't surfed there again, and he hadn't complained about that. We'd surfed at Kuta Reef, and we'd got some good waves. I wondered if I could have helped him at Uluwatu had the situations been reversed. I would have done anything for him, but there was nothing to do for him. He didn't need me, I guess. That thought stuck in my craw. I couldn't shake it, and it started off a sentence in my head that droned, and I hated what it said, but a part of me agreed with it:

You've got to be better than him at something.

They served chicken on the plane. It tasted like fish. By the time we got home I was sick. The chicken-fish came back out tasting like ash. Over the toilet bowl, with my eyes closed, fluorescent pixels and rolling credits danced against my eyelids.

DAY
MINUS
5830

I came back from Bali rangy and unsettled, and feeling like I needed to *do something*. I vandalised the music teacher's van. I ripped off the windscreen wipers, keyed the paint and put a dent in the door with my knee. The music teacher was also the basketball coach, and he had his favourites and I wasn't one of them – I never got time on court.

After the vandalism, I was suspended from school. It confused people, because they thought it was out of character for me. Or that's what they said, with disappointment in their voices. But I liked the surprise in their eyes. A lot of the teachers wanted me to be expelled, but the headmaster held an appeal, and he let me stay because I had done just that one thing wrong and was otherwise a good student.

Dad took me by the shoulders after that appeal, out by his car, and he's a damn sight taller than me so he bent down to look me in the eye.

'Did you see your mother in there?' he asked.

I shook my head.

'She was crying.'

I looked across at her, already in the car.

'We want the best for you,' he said.

He didn't understand why I'd done it and I couldn't explain it to him. Something had just flashed in me and I'd found myself attacking the van. There was anger in it, but also pride and malevolence. This was something I hadn't felt before, and it felt good.

I was obliged to write the music teacher an authentic-sounding letter of apology and repentance. The letter dragged itself out of my pen like the pen was rusty, and it got me my second chance. But a loud part inside me didn't regret the vandalism.

He deserved it, it said.

Afterwards I was treated with suspicion by some disapproving teachers, but the history teacher, Foley, was different. He asked me to join the rugby team and he taught me how to play. I became a good player and Foley told me that, to my face. I remember it. Rugby games wore me out physically, but also built me up with nerves and expectation and satisfaction.

After one Saturday game, Luke and I paddled out to the Point, and when we got out the back he sat up and said, 'Mate, you were the best player out there.'

It meant so much that he said that.

I turned seventeen and had grown from small to big, and this change gave me a quiet confidence. I was full of brimming life, and felt that I had something inside me that was ready for whatever was coming. I'd drive around at night, aimless and fast, and stop at the deserted beach and stand in the grass on the dunes, in the wild night wind, just watching the heavy darkness above the whipping sea.

My school sent a rugby team and a hockey team to New Zealand on a sports trip. On the second night there was a party, and the talk was of a girl called Bec, a new face. The school's hockey team had drafted her in from another local school. She was the star player, almost 6 feet tall, and she surfed, and she was damn good-looking. I caught her eye once, early in the night. Then I got drunk, and towards the end of the party I approached her outside on a dim balcony. She drank alcohol out of a plastic cup with a straw that she held with one hand right up to her mouth. She asked me my name, and then she said, 'I've been wanting this to happen.'

And I said, 'What?'

And we started kissing. She ran her hands over my shoulders, down my sides, and hooked her thumbs under my belt. The feeling of her touch stung in my hands and feet and stayed with me for a long, long time.

My seventeen-year-old synapses didn't have the vocab required to really describe a woman. I was simply staggered. Bec and I stood no further than 2 inches apart until the party ended.

She said, 'I like you.'

Then she left and my mind replayed her saying that, because it was bold and available. It was right there in its honesty; something I had gained unexpectedly and didn't want to lose. For the rest of the tour Bec and I sought each other out, sneaking into back rooms at parties, drinking. We sat together on the bus during long trips and talked. She was the first person I'd ever seen put on lip gloss – she applied it to her top lip and then smooched it onto her bottom lip.

'You want some?'

I said no, but when she looked away I smooched my lips together, and, goddamn, she was alluring to me.

After the tour finished, a pang of jealousy sounded in me like a gong. It tightened my stomach. Bec was going to a party when she got home, her ex-boyfriend was going to be there, did I know him? Yes, I knew the cockhead. He went to my school. He was obsessed with her, apparently, and I could understand that; oh yes, I could.

Bec said, 'Don't worry about him.'

And that's when I got the pang.

Back at school, after the New Zealand tour, people asked me about Bec and I just said that I didn't know much about her. Then she called me one night, and then she called the next night, and the next. And these phone calls became a part of my day that I waited for, and I thought that some of the things she said to me were things she had never told anyone before.

After quite a few of those calls, the phone rang one evening at home and my younger sister, Sarah, rushed to answer it.

'Glenn!' she yelled.

Sarah came to my bedroom door.

'That girl's on the phone for you.'

Sarah giggled and wanted me to laugh too but I kept a straight face. My family were on the couch watching telly and they looked up as I took the phone from the kitchen bench, stepped outside and shut the sliding door against its cord.

Bec said, 'Come over.'

I pulled on my shoes.

'I'm going to Bec's house.'

'Now?'

'Yeah.'

'Aren't you studying?'

'Yeah.'

I closed the door.

I had a chemistry exam the next day, but that night biology took over. Forty minutes to Bec's house, I floored it. Bec opened the door and we lay on her living room floor. She wore shorts and her legs stretched to just up under her nearly exposed bum cheeks; long legs on a bed of beige carpet. I stayed with her until her mother went reluctantly to bed and left us alone. I got home after midnight.

I started driving over to Bec's house a lot, the music blaring, and staying late and feeling a huge momentum powering me. On the drives home, my mind was so occupied with thoughts of her that I'd pull up in the driveway and not remember a second of the trip, not a stop sign, or a car, or a corner, or the sound of the road, not a damn thing, as if I'd been in a dream, on autopilot.

As soon as I earned Bec's trust and love, I stopped trusting her. I started caring for her so much that the joy of being with her was tainted by an intense need to know that she was mine and only mine. The drives to her house became rushed and aggressive. My thoughts ran through scenarios of her betrayal, and it wasn't until I got to her and she was in my sight that I could let myself believe she was only mine.

One Friday night I drove to Bec's place through the bush, along the Ridgeway Road, and stopped at a dilapidated servo. I could smell the clutch and I shook my head. I hated my Ford Laser hatch, with its shabby, cat-vomited-on interior, its decaying silver paint-job, and its boring front-wheel drive. The service station was dimly lit. Shadows cast themselves around the pumps and gathered on the road. I pumped fuel into the Laser.

The Ridgeway was a dirt road and mud spat up by the wheels had dried on the side of the car. I tapped it with my foot and it slid off in clumps. My brother Tim was in the car; I was dropping him at a party. He sat motionless. He hadn't said a word. Even when I raced up to blind corners, swinging onto the wrong side of the road, he had been quiet.

The numbers on the petrol pump flipped over, and their slowness made me furious. I wanted another car. Goddamn, what I needed was a Hilux. There was a guy from down the road who drove me to school sometimes, Tanner – he had a Hilux. A car that he'd swing off Tumbi Road onto Bellevue Road with the back end fishtailing on the gravel. He'd correct wildly to the right and then less wildly to the left, and as the back end of the Hilux straightened he'd slip it into third. He was the least likely candidate for that shit – mild, unassuming Tanner, of all people. I wanted to drive like Tanner. I wanted to lose control and casually regain it. I wanted to impress like Tanner had impressed me. The Laser wouldn't slide; even on the Ridgeway, where the gradient was steep and the curves sharp, it was hard to impress my brother in it. I'd made a mistake in buying that car. I'd accepted reasonable arguments about its cheapness, its parking attributes, its petrol economy. I shook my head.

What a shitbox.

If I could go back in time, I'd tell the kid I was that the anger behind his confidence was what also made him selfish; it had trapped him in his head and made him blind to what was outside. I'd drive the Laser away from him and leave him to walk home in the dark and think, and that would be a mercy for that kid. But there's no going back in time, except for in the mind. Sometimes it's possible to forgive mistakes that way and sometimes it's not.

I paid for the petrol and walked back to my Laser, gravel crunching underfoot. I drove onto the road and under the heaving canopy. The headlights sharpened against approaching cliffs and the other side of the road dropped away into swirling bush. I drove fast. Descending off the ridge, houses on acreages began popping up between the trees. They flashed by. On a sweeping right-hand bend, I thought, *Too fast.*

I lost control. The conclusion was fixed before I could get my foot on the brake. The wheels slid, the steering locked and we ran off the road and over an embankment that fell towards trees. I heard tyres skid and saw headlights swing into the sky. The car rolled onto its side. Branches rushed against the doors. I gripped the wheel. The trees came, and then stopped. Stones and dirt rained on the car, making the sound of wind through leaves. White tree trunks stood around like the legs of giants. The car was tipped at 70 degrees, the engine dead, the right front wheel above me spinning.

I undid my seatbelt. I found the door handle but it wouldn't open.

I turned my head slowly on a robot neck. Tim was facing me. And he was quiet and just waiting for me to be quiet, and for me to look at him. His face was mostly in the dark and for a moment I thought his eyes were frozen and unblinking. That's what I remember. Tim was a sensitive soul, a beautiful brother who I ignored, and he was staring at me now, with big trees around us.

'Are you alright?' I mumbled.

He looked down.

'I think so,' he replied.

I felt okay. That's how selfish I was.

'We missed the trees,' he said.

The rolling of the car and the thick lantana had slowed our descent and stopped us before the trees. People who lived nearby had heard the skid and ran out of their houses. They thought we were dead. They said that people had died on that corner before. I hoped they wouldn't ring the police, and they didn't.

Luke arrived to help me. I knew I was in a situation he would never end up in. Looking at the car crumpled up, I felt stupid – but also exhilarated by this stupid thing. I'd thought that I was just some imperfect clone of Luke, but this was outside the scope of a clone. I was actually someone else entirely, and I felt some strange glee at being someone he would never be.

I called a tow truck to drag the Laser out of the ditch. With a practised self-absorption, I worried about the car; I hated it, but it was all I had. It was dinged, and it wouldn't start. The tow truck driver said to leave it right side up for a while.

I looked at Tim. He'd been only good to me. And I wanted to put my arm around his shoulders and ask if he was okay, but I didn't do it. I just watched the car leak oil onto the road.

'That was the only corner you took slow,' he said.

Tim's words broke my solipsism. I saw some adult thing in his face I hadn't seen before. It made no sense to me then; my inward self didn't recognise that Tim understood me better than I understood myself. He had already become a man, right out from under me. Someone organised to drive him away, I don't know who.

My car was towed home. I pulled the branches out of the grill. It started again, and I willed myself to forget the accident.

During that year of being seventeen, I decided that I wanted to become a great rugby player, and I believed that it was possible. I started surfing better than I had, catching sets from the crowd. I thought it would be impossible for me to get fat; if I got fat I would run until I wasn't – I'd run until I vomited. During my final high school exams I studied for six hours a day. I got a sick joy from it. The exams were easy and I was accepted into environmental science at Newcastle University; I'd applied on the basis that the environment was becoming a societal preoccupation and studies of it would be, doubtless, lucrative. I would move from the Central Coast to Newcastle. My future had taken shape effortlessly. My daydreams were clear and attainable. I was hungry. I was pumped with life. And I had Bec.

Then it started to unravel.

The police called. I'd been reported for reckless driving and they wanted my licence, but Dad intervened and I was only warned. He asked me what the hell I'd been doing. Every time I looked at Tim, the car crash came back to me like a nightmare. I'd not been able to repress the memory of the crash, and I realised that if I had hurt him I would have been so sickened, I would have wanted to kill myself. I had dreams of him speared by a tree. It became the most shameful moment of my life.

Then my mother suggested that I was unhealthily infatuated with Bec.

'What!'

'You never see your friends.'

I stormed away.

Bad, true things brought unexpectedly to light always hurt to hear. I was struggling with Luke as well. He had been tolerant of Bec, but indifferent too. We just didn't talk about her, but Jawbone openly patronised her, while also implying that I had become servile to her, and Luke laughed sincerely at his 'you're so pussy-whipped' jokes. Bec's presence was clearly an inconvenience to Luke. And it was only me that wanted everyone to just get along. I was in love with her, and I couldn't stand the way Luke's eyes rolled when she arrived. I wished I didn't know the words running through his head: *Here we fucken go.*

The tension between Bec, Luke and I developed into a flattened isosceles triangle, with me trying to be equally close to both of them and them trying to be as far away from each other as possible. The tension tightened lips and stilted conversations, and their joint presence became uncomfortable and rare. It soured everything. It shitted me that Luke wouldn't even make one sacrifice for me and just fucking like her. I saw less of him; I made excuses to avoid watching cricket all day, or hanging out at the Bay Village eating doughnuts and checking out chicks, and a small distance grew between us that stretched into a large gap until it became hard to close. Despite this, though, I always thought we'd be best mates. I never believed our friendship would change.

One afternoon in the summer of 1993, I was with Bec and her friends drinking in the Terrigal Beer Garden. Bec and I were very close, and she was going to move with me when I went to Newcastle for university. I thought we would always be together.

That night she told her friends, 'I'm wearing my boyfriend skirt.'

It was a long brown skirt that went all the way to her ankles. Bec had started wearing more conservative clothing, because I was not coping with other blokes looking at her. I insisted on the longer skirts.

The Beer Garden was buzzing and full of my school friends. Luke was there with Jawbone.

'Hey,' I said.

He nodded and sipped his beer, then looked away, bored and cold. I turned. Jawbone was walking towards the bar and he glanced back at Luke, a Cheshire grin on his face, and some unspoken joke passed between them that I knew was about me. I turned back towards Luke. He was rolling his eyes and making a face that I can name, now, as contempt, but back then I took to simply mean, *What a fuckwit.*

Luke saw me, and saw I was furious, and my reaction made him laugh. Our friendship began to burn out then. It was clear to me that I was no longer his best mate, that there'd been a replacement. I couldn't accept that. It was a small thing, a tiny moment in a long friendship, but I decided to make no further effort. If I saw Luke, I saw him, but I wasn't going out of my way.

Despite this, there was, for a while, a keeping up of appearances – we had an occasional beer, a surf, he dropped me at university one time. But our conversations didn't go easy ever again. We were both unwilling to admit to any fault, and there was a stubbornness in both of us that the other found impenetrable. Our time together grew into periods of silence, and these silences were not acknowledged and nor was the resentment that came with them. Our friendship suffocated. I watched it happening, and I was silent and stoic and too angry to feel any sadness. I, like him, never wanted to show any signs of weakness.

DAY
MINUS
5500

One evening my sister came to my bedroom door and said, 'We just saw Bec.'

I looked up from my book.

'She looked happy,' said Sarah.

'Happy? Did you speak to her? '

'No, I just saw her with her friends, a girl and some guys.'

'Guys?'

'Yeah. So?'

'Nothing,' I said. Sarah walked off.

What guys? How could she be happy?

Bec and I were in the middle of a three-day argument. At the start of this argument, she had thrown my Big Mac out the car window. And in the rear-view mirror I saw my burger smeared on the pavement and I stopped talking. I pulled up at her place and all I said was, 'Get out.'

And I sped off, certain that I had the upper hand. I had stormed away in high dudgeon and Bec ought to have been crushed. She should have been crying into her pillow, and wishing that I would stop the silent treatment and let her apologise for wronging me.

I was unable to communicate during arguments. Storming out was the one good tool I had, and I relied on it wholly. Then I instituted a silent treatment. It was a tyrannical combination. After three days of silence I would waver, but usually three days was enough for the carcass of my victim to stiffen and for me to pounce on it and reap my revenge for its wrong, wrong, wrongness. But now I was hearing that Bec was hanging out with guys.

I drove to Bec's place. Her car wasn't there.

Wronged.

It got dark. Headlights lined up at a distant traffic light on the highway. The wind dropped and crickets sounded. I got out of my car and leaned against it. I was wearing tattered grey tracksuit pants, ugg boots and an unwashed black jumper. I wasn't dressing so good; I didn't have to. I pulled the hood of my jumper over my head, and my fury began to subside. I got cold, and tired, and really I just wanted the argument to end. The night was black by then. A faraway streetlight shone off the tar.

Bec's Torana pulled into the driveway, its headlights bright. She got out of the car and I stepped out of a shadow.

'Hi,' she said, surprised.

'Where have you been?'

She shrugged. 'With some friends.'

'Which friends?'

'Just *friends*, Glenn.'

We stood there in silence. 'I just want to stop arguing,' I said.

'Let's go inside,' she said.

We went into Bec's bedroom. It had become my second home. I liked the smell, its cleanliness, the set of drawers I'd painted, the hockey sticks in the corner. She began to cry.

'It's okay, Bec. I'm not that angry.'

'It's not that.'

She paused.

'I don't love you any more,' she told me.

That didn't feel right.

She repeated it. It took a while to sink in, because I was caught off guard. I was confused, blindsided.

'What about moving to Newcastle?'

'I don't want to.'

I realised we were not going to be together forever. My lips trembled. I tried not to cry, but the tears rushed me and rolled down my cheeks. I wiped them away, staring at their traces on the heel of my palm, warm and unstoppable. She covered her mouth, her eyes brimming.

'It's okay,' I said.

The thing I didn't say was, *You are all I've got.*

I didn't need to say that. She knew that.

We hugged at her front door. I drove home without seeing the road or the approaching headlights, without being present for a second of that drive. I walked into my parents' bedroom and told them. My mother cried. I felt desolate. Eventually I went into my bedroom, which I had barely slept in for a year.

My post-relationship relationship with Bec was torture. She was happy. I was not. She moved on. I did not. She wore short skirts and saw other men, and everyone told me about it, and it ripped up my sinew.

'Are you sure this is what you want?' I asked her.

'Yes,' she said. 'Totally.'

I couldn't understand why. I begged her to meet me on Valentine's Day. I waited for her, with a picnic, until it got dark and the mozzies came, and she never turned up.

My future lost shape and form. I met this one person at uni, a sexy, totally unavailable Goth girl with white makeup and black lipstick who never smiled. She told me that my environmental science degree wouldn't be worth anything more than toilet paper, and this opinion gave voice to my own unconscious doubts, and I dropped out. Reality was difficult.

Back in Terrigal again, I got an all-night pizza delivery job paying three dollars a pizza. I took a long time on my deliveries, making detours past Bec's house to check if her car was home – not out; I didn't want it out. Who would she be out with? That pizza job – driving, slicing warm pizza into contiguous eighths, watching fights on The Entrance Road – was sometimes just enough to stop me thinking about Bec and her coldness, and the disbelief that ran around in my mind so fast that I had to shake my head to stop it for a moment. At midnight, after shutting off the pizza oven and the lights, I'd sink into a plastic chair and drink bourbon cans while the very early morning got quieter and quieter.

My parents had anticipated the disaster with Bec and had tried to warn me. I felt stupid that I had been so wrong. My parents were good to me. They tried to make it easier. Dad told me that he wished he could have my heartbreak for me, so that I wouldn't have to go through it. Mum encouraged me to keep busy. She told me, 'You're living life, Glenn. This is it – real feelings and emotions. You're really living.'

I didn't get it.

My parents suggested that I keep a low profile and save up for the next university year, as I'd reapplied. Instead, I went crazy. I argued with Bec. I tried to make her jealous. I danced close to Trish, the pizza shop manager, at a nightclub to make Bec jealous. She didn't notice. I saw her kiss the DJ, and I yelled abuse at her. A friend pulled me away.

I had no control over my anger – it was wild and without bounds. I blamed her and I blamed the world.

The next day, my father sat me down.

'Bec's mother is threatening to call the police,' he said.

I was ashamed he had to deal with this.

'You're about to start university, again,' Dad said. 'Just stay at home. Don't go out.'

DAY
MINUS
5200

Although I had dropped out of university, I'd paid a full year of membership to the student union, and so was allowed to join the Newcastle University rugby club. I made the second-grade team and drove up to Newcastle three times a week for training and games. It was a ninety-minute drive each way, which gave me a lot of time to think – too much. I didn't know how to stop my mind's sad chatter. Nirvana, Guns N' Roses and Pearl Jam cassettes lay scattered on the floor of my car, while I listened to The Pretenders – that's how sad it got. Those drives were the end of my adolescence, the end of a time when anger overwhelmed everything, and the start of a time when reality cracked over me as a sadness that I could not cast off.

Every week to begin with, I took my surfboard with me on those drives to Newcastle and stopped at North Entrance to check the waves. I leaned on a green pine fence that bordered the car park, spinifex shaking around it, and watched the ocean. I didn't go out. It always looked shit on those wintry afternoons. It was dribbly mush, or it broke too fast, or there were too many guys out. Surfing and my friendship with Luke had always been a package, and now that he was gone, much was also gone from my love of the sport. It was spoiled. Surfing by myself sucked. Eventually I stopped taking my board and stopped looking at the surf, and just drove right on.

I'd joined the uni rugby club because I wanted to be good at something. I wasn't expecting to make friends. Despite that, after my first game, in a stinking, cramped changing shed, a player introduced himself.

'Damo,' he said. 'How'd you pull up?'

Damo and I had a beer and he introduced me to his two mates, Mud and Larko. We sat in the stand and watched the first-grade team run on, and I wanted to be in that first-grade team. I drove home and worked all night delivering pizzas with rugby socks in the back of the car and sore legs.

Rugby training was on Tuesday and Thursday nights. I'd arrive early, park in the outside lot, switch off my headlights, and wait. I'd watch the ground lighting come on slowly, and see the players arrive and mill, laugh, talk. I'd slip down low in my seat, not wanting to be seen. I had one question for myself: *Why are you in your car, in the dark, with some really sensitive music playing, when everyone else is being social?*

I had to force myself out of the car.

When Damo arrived, and Mud and Larko, they talked animatedly about getting back to college in time to watch *Melrose Place*, because the chick ratio was two to one in the TV room when *Melrose* was on. And after training there was a rush from the oval, car doors opening and slamming.

'Who's coming?'

Cars sped away towards the dark hills beyond the oval, the air full of their hooting. Their enthusiasm affected me, and I started thinking that it might be a good thing to live at a college like they did. And there came a time on one of those drives back to the Central Coast after training when I asked myself if I wasn't sick of that Pretenders tape, and I turned it off. And I felt a little less heartsore.

As that rugby season neared its end, Damo said to me, 'What are you doing next year?'

'Not sure.'

'You should do engineering.'

And that was why I applied to do engineering.

'You should join my college,' said Damo. 'It's awesome.'

And that was why I applied to his college.

I didn't know then that Damo had a soft spot for stray people. He was wise, I guess. Who knows how, at twenty-two? Once, drunk, he said to me, 'You know, Gorgo, you're not a very fucken well-rounded person, mate.'

I didn't believe that at the time; I didn't realise what a clever bastard he was.

At the end of the season, Damo, Mud and Larko convinced me to go with them to the Crown and Anchor Hotel in central New-castle on a Saturday night. It was packed with rugby players. The windows were steamed up and smoke and song poured out of an open door. I knew the people in there by nickname: Evil Dave, Jam-mer, Lomax, Binnie, Gee and Newie; Marcho, Mailo and Army; Pritch and XB. I stood just on the inside, squashed against the glass, four deep from a horseshoe bar. A free beer came to me. I skolled it. A song started, loud, and its vile lyrics stopped pedestrians walk-ing by outside. Another beer came. I drank it. I got drunk in twenty minutes. I stumbled in a crowd. Late in the night I stood outside a shop eating hot chips from a paper bag, then later I stood in a sta-tionary crowd near a road, and it was cold, and I said to the guy next to me, 'What are we waiting for?'

He wiped his mouth and I saw that it was Damo, and he gig-gled. The road in front of us went a long way in both directions and a bus came from one of those directions. The bus took us some-where, and there I found my car and slept in it.

When I arrived at college to live, I was allotted a small room. My parents checked the cupboards.

'They've got tea here,' said Dad.

I nodded.

'You want a cup of tea?'

I shook my head.

'No,' said Mum. 'He wants us to go.'

I was quiet, not wanting them to think I didn't want them there.

'It's okay, honey,' she said. She hugged me.

I sat on the bed looking at the blank brick wall.

I've left the Coast behind.

And I said to myself, *There is nothing there anyway.*

But I watched Dad's car pulling out of the car park and knew that in some ways the Coast would always be home, and that some of the people there meant everything.

I walked through the halls of the college. I said g'day to strangers. From snippets of conversation, I heard that there had been a massive party the night before. I ventured into the dining hall and took a tray filled with sloppy food. I looked for an empty table.

'Hey, mate,' said someone.

'Who are you?' they asked.

'Glenn.'

'How come we haven't seen you?'

'I just arrived.'

I sat down. Chairs around me filled. People were introduced. Girl after girl walked through the room. The place became electric.

Over that year, I trained hard and made it into the uni first-grade rugby team, and I lived for Saturday nights at the Crown and Anchor. And I felt like I had found a place that was right for me.

DAY
MINUS
4100

When university holidays came, I went back to the Coast out of money. I worked at a waterslide that was dilapidated and bleak, and nobody came. Working there sapped my energy, and eventually the place went broke and closed down. Then I got a job in a Mexican restaurant, washing dishes, and it didn't pay much, and it sucked. So I decided to sell the Laser. It had finally turned into a total piece of shit. It had always been a prick of a wagon, but now it also had a lot of rust and the paint was peeling. I asked Tim to help me repaint it; he was good with cars. Outside the garage we sat on warm concrete with sandpaper and primer surrounding us.

'Hold this,' he said.

Tim drilled a hole into a dent on the door panel. He inserted an L-shaped tool into the hole, pulled gently, and the depression popped out.

'Good work,' I said.

'Easy.'

'Do you reckon it will take me long to do the rest?'

The Laser was half-sanded, dented, shabby.

'Weeks,' he replied. 'How much are you going to sell it for?'

'A grand.'

'Then when you go back to uni you won't have to call.'

'Huh?'

'The only reason you call is to ask for money.'

'That's not true.'

'That's what Mum and Dad think.'

'How would you know?'

'That's what they think.'

He walked off.

I started thinking about my siblings. Tim was seventeen by then, and Richard and Sarah were both fifteen. All the time I'd been away at uni I hadn't spoken with them, not one letter or phone call. And now that I was back, it was kind of creepy and intriguing to see them assessing me as they would a stranger.

I walked inside. They were lying about the lounge room. They all loved music; that was their thing, concerts and music. Tim played guitar, Richard drums and Sarah was a singer. I picked up Tim's guitar and plucked at it, and he winced.

'What are you doing?'

On the stereo was the song 'I Could Have Lied' by Red Hot Chili Peppers.

'How do you play this?' I asked.

'It's pretty hard, Glenn.'

'How do you play it?'

Tim showed me how to play a chord. I pursed my lips tightly and manipulated my fingers into the right positions. They watched, slightly amused, and on their faces was the question: *What's he doing this for?*

I persevered. After a while they were all wincing.

TWANG.

Over the summer I learnt the introduction to 'I Could Have Lied'. I dedicated hours to it, it was the only song I listened to. Tim and Richard had 'jams' on guitar and drums, and I chimed in with 'I Could Have Lied' (which rarely worked). I grew my hair long, like them. I was friendly to their friends. I laid off the big-brotherly slap-downs. I escorted Sarah to her high school formal and loved her better than I had.

Late that summer, Tim and I went to the Livid Festival in Brisbane. He thought I could buy a ticket at the gate and I drove twelve hours with him to Brisbane, and there were no tickets left at the gate. So Tim boosted me over the wire fence at 7 a.m. and I hid in a portaloo until the festival started. Then we watched Regurgitator and smoked Tim's marijuana pipe. When Everclear came on, we pushed through the crowd. Tim lifted me up high and for a few seconds I surfed across the heaving crowd, my Doc Martens blocking and unblocking the sun, the guitar riff thumping in my chest. And for a long time after that day I could close my eyes and remember those seconds exactly as they had been, as magical, and I thought it was the band, the sun, the crowd. But it wasn't that; it was Tim, and because we had gotten closer.

In early 1995, a Newcastle team was invited to play in the Sydney rugby competition and Mud and I trialled for the under-twenties team. Mud was a good guy; likeable, grounded. His nickname had only stuck because it was the opposite of reality – he was clean-cut and admired, and it was really me and my name that, with the under-twenties coach at least, was mud.

Making the under-twenties team became important to me. I got very serious. If I made mistakes at training or in a game, it bothered me for days. The coach slogged us harder than I'd ever been slogged in a preseason, and I didn't like the coach and he didn't like me; it was a personality clash. He believed that he was a boxer of some note. I was not at all impressed by that. I thought he was a skivvy-wearing idiot. Despite this, I was close to making the team. A squad of forty had been whittled down to twenty-five, of which they would pick twenty-two.

At a night training session the coach sent Mud and me down the field to receive kicks. He wanted us to catch his kick and run it back to be tackled by an eight-man forward pack. I looked at Mud.

'What's the point of this?'

We wandered down the darkened field. The coach kicked. The ball went straight up, it made no sound, and still I heard it turning over in the air. I got under the ball and caught it. I didn't even take a step. I was swamped by eight tacklers. One around my legs, another hit me in the middle; my arms were trapped. A forward from Maitland swung his forearm across my face as the tacklers piled on. Hot blood ran over my lips. After a while the coach blew his whistle.

'Don't bleed on me,' someone said.

I had played with some of the Maitland forwards in the NSW Country trials the year before. They hadn't wanted to shake hands with the opposition, considering it weak. Mud and I thought that was bullshit and said so, and I guess it had left some resentment.

I got onto my knees. My eyes were bleary and blood ran through my fingers. The coach sent everyone to the scrum machine.

'You'd better go,' he told me.

I walked away, hearing the sound of a whistle and yelling near the grandstand where the senior team trained, and went back into the dressing sheds. A club official was massaging the leg of a distinguished senior player.

'You alright?' he asked.

I got my bag and walked home. I iced my nose, and then gingerly inserted tissue into my nostrils. The bleeding stopped, but my nose was blocked from rim to brain.

There was another player competing for my position in the team. He was from Maitland, too, and he was quick. I knew I would have to play in the last two games to have a chance of making the team. My nose was broken. I knew that. It was crooked.

I have to make the team.

Mud came home. I closed my bedroom door.

I grew anxious and a headache started. In a moment of weakness I called Bec.

'Why are you calling?'

'I broke my nose.'

'Are you okay?'

'Yeah.'

'What's the matter?'

I hadn't spoken to her for a long time. I tried to tell her what had happened, and to explain about the past, but it came out in a faltering tremor and I had to say goodbye.

The next day I stayed home. I didn't hear from the coach.

Dad organised for me to see a doctor, who took an x-ray.

'You have a deviated septum.'

'Is it broken?'

'Yes.'

'Will I have to get it fixed?'

'Well, you can. You would need surgery. How is your breathing?'

'It's better today.'

'And you're a rugby player?'

'Yeah.'

'And you want to keep playing?'

'Yeah.'

'In that case, don't get it fixed. You'll only break it again. If you can breathe, it's just the way it looks you'll have to deal with.'

'Can I play this weekend?'

He wriggled his nose.

'I'd give it a week.'

The next night I went to training. The guy who broke my nose came over to me.

'Sorry,' he said with a crooked smile.

My coach didn't say anything. The young Maitland player who was competing for the same position as me laughed.

'Mate, we hoped you weren't coming back.'

It sounded like a joke, but there was truth in it as well.

I played that weekend. I felt sluggish, and I didn't do much right or much wrong. Then in the last game I played well – I scored two tries – and the Maitland guy played shit. I thought I had done enough to get in the side.

On the afternoon the team was being announced, the coach called me at home.

'I'm dropping you,' he told me.

My heart sank.

'Why?'

'I don't like the way you've been playing.'

There was no point in arguing.

I walked outside onto the road, in front of the share house I'd recently moved into. From there I could see Newcastle harbour, sunlit, but underneath the sparkle it was dark like ash. I squatted down and watched it for a long time until clouds came over and everything went grey.

The next year I didn't do much preseason rugby training. I didn't really care if I was a good player. There was a relief in not trying. I played at the NSW Country carnival in Dubbo; there were NSW Country under-21 selectors watching and that was the lure of playing. But then I got so drunk the night before that I barely made it to our game, arriving hungover to pull on my boots for the second half. We lost.

The year after that I didn't do any preseason training. I spent the summer playing guitar, and working as a student engineer at Shell's Clyde refinery. I didn't enjoy rugby at all that year, and only liked the drinking on Saturday nights. On other nights I felt melancholy as I went to sleep. I told myself it would go away. But sometimes I woke up in the morning and the melancholy was still there. I read a story about a girl who could only see the colour green, and I felt that I understood the sensation of everything being the same. It bothered me that I had a constant dreariness weighing on me and I tried to rationalise it as boredom, but it wasn't. It wasn't anything I had a name for then.

DAY MINUS 2100

I first saw Elizabeth at The Grand, an old hotel with a front bar, which they called the public bar, for hard liquor, and a back bar, which they called the private bar (but which was actually public), for beer and pool. It had tiled walls and was heavily fogged with cigarette smoke.

On Saturday nights I'd arrive there late, stumbling, with ten other rugby players and we'd wedge our way into the crowd, someone yelling loud whose shout it was. And one Saturday night, there was Elizabeth in the corner, with short dark hair and big eyes. From the corner of my eye I watched her, and she'd glance over, then give a tiny smile, and turn around and sip her drink.

And again, later: glance, look down, sip.

Ha. What's this bullshit?

She was too difficult. I was plastered. Where were the easy roots?

A yell in my face: 'It's your *shout*.'

A beer half full. A glass tipping up and flowing out its last foam. A meat pie. Soggy chips. Living room carpet, flat out, *Rage*, snoring, sleepy sounds.

Not long after that night, my flatmate Dave approached Elizabeth's clique at The Grand. He withstood a salvo of their mockery and made a witty retort that had them in stitches. Dave introduced me to Elizabeth. She pretended that we'd never seen each other before. We talked in a combative way that was disdainful but friendly.

Then I asked her out to the movies and while we were there I spilt Coke all over her. I, by then rather uncomfortable, apologised at each lull during the movie. Eventually she told me to get over it.

Nothing much happened after that date. There was no flaming passion, but there was a genuine warmth, an organic heat. Before that, at university, I'd had only meaningless flings, nothing serious. If seriousness threatened I would melt away.

To start with, Elizabeth and I saw each other only occasionally, mostly at a pub accompanied by other friends. I liked her but felt a wavering, a withdrawal. The emotional drama with Bec had scarred me, although I probably didn't recognise that at the time. But after several weeks of seeing occasionally but not quite dating Elizabeth, she looked me in the eyes and her eyes said, *Well, I'm here, and you're here, and you know that I think we're boyfriend and girlfriend even though it hasn't been agreed, and you are on thin ice with me and it's thinning further.*

Elizabeth liked cafes. I didn't drink coffee; its rich, bitter smell nauseated me. I could only order childish beverages, like hot chocolates or milkshakes; it was undignified. Elizabeth started serious, sober conversations with me, and in that way she was the first woman I'd ever really known.

'What are you doing after uni?' she asked.

'I don't know.'

My friends were going overseas, but I had no interest in that. My future had no shape. Elizabeth looked into her mugaccino and I gathered that I should have said something about 'us'. She had life plans and desires. I didn't think we would work out.

That same night, or the next, or the one after, I got tinnitus – a ringing in the ears that never stops. There is no cure. My dad got it in his
twenties and I followed suit. Tinnitus can drive people nuts. It can
lead to depression, anxiety and sleep problems. It woke me up the
first time I noticed it. Elizabeth was there and told me to go back to
sleep, but in the morning the ringing wasn't gone. It stayed for days,
then weeks, and the doctor told me it would never go away. I turned
the TV up loud, but nothing blocked it out. I stopped sleeping.

'Don't concentrate on it,' said Dad. 'Just let it be there.'

'I don't have to let it *be*,' I said, angrily. 'It is there.'

'Relax. Accept it.'

Why me?

That question tortured me. It seemed so unfair that the world
had made this thing in me. I broke down. Elizabeth was there,
listening and understanding me in a way I'd never felt with Bec.
She helped me accept the ringing. I taught myself to stop thinking
about it. I learnt what 'let it be' meant.

And by then things had changed between Elizabeth and me.
She'd become my girlfriend.

When university ended, Damo went to Ireland, Mud went to Amer-
ica, and Shell offered me a reservoir engineering job in Holland with
a ridiculously good salary, and I accepted.

'That is amazing! I am so excited for you,' said Elizabeth.

I was not excited. I felt like a liar and a bore. I was only mildly
enthusiastic, marginally convinced, running like a detuned engine.
Nothing felt high or low. Elizabeth had become my closest friend.
I told her I loved her and I meant it, but I also knew instinctively
that it was missing something.

I was due in Holland in February, so I had three months to kill.
I said goodbye to Newcastle and packed my shit. Elizabeth moved

to Sydney, and I stayed with her. We couldn't decide what was going to happen with us. It was a difficult question.

That summer Elizabeth and I went to the beach most weekends. She lay flat out under the rays while I swam in the waves. And those days were fun and easy, but they also came with unease, with both of us knowing that I was leaving soon.

December and January rolled over me quickly, and a taxi arrived in February to take me to the airport. I felt okay, just a slight sadness. I said goodbye to my parents. Elizabeth hugged me, and I felt a rush of emotion that I fought to repress. There was a possibility that she would join me overseas, but nothing was decided. Elizabeth hung on to my mum; my mum knows how to take care of people.

I was booked in business class, but my seat was taken by a seasoned-looking traveller. The engines started. A flight attendant came. The lady in my seat unlocked her belt and began stuffing shit in her handbag.

'I'll go,' she said.

'It's okay,' I replied.

I moved on and the lady gave me a hard stare. A curtain was opened by a beautiful flight attendant. 'Sir, we are sorry for any inconvenience.'

I stepped into first class.

'No inconvenience,' I said.

I was mildly happy. When the plane took off, I watched Sydney drift below enormous clouds.

I bounced my legs up and down.

Don't get sad.

I saw Elizabeth crying. I gripped the armrest. Tears came into my eyes and I rubbed them away, embarrassed.

It'll be alright.

It was zero degrees in Holland when I got there, and overcast and bleak. I wandered around The Hague with some other new Shell employees.

'Well,' said one of them, in front of a sex museum, 'we're expats now.'

I was required to attend engineering classes to learn how to drill oil wells. Most days I woke at 5 a.m. in a tiny one-bedroom loft apartment in suburban Scheveningen, in the dark, with snow on the roads. I showered under a tepid drizzle, and put on three layers of clothes, and caught a tram to the Shell learning centre. The classes were complicated, the workload was intense. Late at night, I would hit the piss. I lived on a few hours sleep.

The months blurred until I woke up on a snowy Saturday afternoon, tired and hungover, and I opened a letter from Elizabeth. She loved me, and missed me, and this reminded me of everything I didn't have with me. I felt black. I rolled onto my side and pulled a blanket up to my chin.

An expat now.

It wasn't right for me. I already knew that. I called Elizabeth every day. I wanted to be with her, but I also knew that if she came to Europe we would have to live together. I was twenty-three, and she was twenty-two. I didn't know if it would work out. But she had started thinking about coming over, and when she said, 'Glenn, I'm going to quit my job,' I felt relief.

But then when she said, 'I've booked my ticket,' I was confused.

What am I doing?

And before she got on the plane to Europe, she told me, 'I love you.'

And I said, 'I love you too.'

But it did not burn brightly in me, and I knew it, and that brought sadness.

Shell transferred me to the south-east of England. Elizabeth and I lived there for a few years. To make some new friends I joined a rugby club and it took me all over the country: Penzance, London, Newcastle. I was away on weekends and hitting the piss with twenty-five rugby players. Elizabeth spent those weekends alone, and there were problems with that. There was her loneliness, that was my fault, and also her sense of an emptiness in our relationship that no manner of hard work or discussion would fill. She started feeling resentful and this fuelled our disagreements, and caused our arguments to become explosive and destructive.

When we moved back to Sydney towards the end of 2000, we talked about this and decided to give things one more go. We found a very small apartment in Manly that Elizabeth loved, and we both got busy with our careers. She worked hard so I often got home before her, and I would come into the small apartment and stand in the dark, in the kitchen, and do a 360-degree turn. I could see into every single room: kitchen, living room, main bedroom, bathroom, spare room. If I closed one eye I could see into the bedroom, and when I closed it and opened the other I could see into the living room; bedroom, living room, bedroom, living room.

During our dinners Elizabeth always had one searing, repetitive (and possibly rhetorical) question: 'What are you searching for?'

I'd then cover my face with my hand and press fingers into my eyes, feeling the jelly in my eyeballs bobble. It was muggy in that apartment. Little itchy things jumped on my skin. My response formulated in my mind: *I hate the smallness of this apartment. Seriously, I can see every room at once. I find it irritating and everything in here intrudes on my thoughts.*

But I'd only say, 'I am not *searching* for anything.'

'You're an unhappy person.'

I'd roll my eyes.

'I don't need this. This is pointless.'

She'd point her fork at me.

'What are you passionate about?'

Silence.

'Anything?' she'd ask.

No answer.

'You know,' she said, 'you can be full of life, but most of the time you live inside your head, and it's really sad. What are you always thinking about?'

'Nothing.'

'Rubbish! You're living another life in there. I don't know what you want, Glenn. You're healthy and loved. You're luckier than so many others. Look at your job – you're successful. Isn't that enough?'

'It doesn't mean anything.'

'My God. What do you *want?*'

'I don't know . . . I want to be good at something.'

'Get on with life.'

I rubbed my face. Her fork clinked against the plate as she ate. I looked around.

'From right here,' I said, 'I can see every room in this apartment.'

Elizabeth began talking about us buying an apartment together. I resisted, and these discussions turned into long, taut silences. At some point I gave up arguing with her. I just crossed my arms, adopted a blank face and grunted – stock-standard emotional withdrawal. It seemed to make things easier for me.

Every night I came home and went straight into the spare room to play guitar, or to write, while she watched TV. We went out separately on weekends and arrived home after midnight. Sometimes I stopped on the way home to buy a pie. And one night I saw her in the pie shop at 2 a.m., talking to a man. I didn't know him, but he liked her, I could tell. She looked happy. I felt sorry for us then.

We didn't have moments like that between us any more.

Elizabeth turned and saw me, and smiled. There was no surprise on her face, just a little sadness. I smiled back. Despite all our disputes, underneath the angst she was my best friend. But by then I knew it was time for us to break up. I just couldn't figure out how to do it.

One night I was lying on the couch and Elizabeth came over and hugged me.

This is what I'm giving up, I thought. *This tenderness, this stability.*

I looked out the window of the apartment and watched the Manly ferry steam off towards Sydney Harbour. I held her for a while. We had been together for seven years. I was twenty-eight.

We broke up a few nights later.

DAY
MINUS
1600

After Elizabeth and I broke up in 2003, I encountered long drifts of alone time. *I need this*, I thought.

My mother said, 'Now you'll find out who you are.'

Who I am? Who am *I?*

Perhaps I was another person: a person with passion; a person who could go to sleep and wake up feeling refreshed rather than melancholy; a person with repressed talents. I felt excited.

My friends were all in serious relationships, they had couple lives to live, and so I fell in with an ever-changing cloud of single people: acquaintances, business connections, clients and randoms. Somehow, without much effort, I could relate to these people. I just came to like them, this Cloud of beings. They were optimists – heartbreak? What the fuck was that? The Cloud were satisfied and content; they were free, self-assured, confident people. I wanted their aura of invincibility.

The Cloud were at every bar. Everybody knew them. They were at the flash nightclubs and they liked champagne. I fell in with this Cloud. We did one thing a lot: went out to drink white Russians and chase women.

I need it . . .

I felt strongly that there was a part of my twenties I had lost to my long-term relationship with Elizabeth. I wanted to salvage it. I wanted the thrill of the chase. I didn't actually want to know any of the women I was chasing; I just needed to prove that I could get them. It became my challenge, some kind of substitute for passion. I was fixated. I see, now, that I was judging myself by my reflection in others, and I had started to think of picking up women as a satisfying lifestyle.

Why would I live any other way, when I can just screw chicks on the weekends with no responsibility?

That was fulfilment. Every girl I slept with was a reassurance. It was easy to like myself when someone else wanted me. I was heartless. I promised all and delivered nothing; beneath a veneer of compassion was my ego. When I'd had enough, I jettisoned, dismissed; a fuck, a phone call, break up and then forget. Forget, forget, forget, and never look back. It was easy, meaningless, every man for himself.

One Saturday morning at 3 a.m. in Kings Cross, when I had just turned twenty-nine, I was drunk, bleeding and humiliated, my shirt ripped open. I argued with two transvestites about a cab that had just pulled up on Bayswater Road. They told me to fuck off.

I'd been in a fight at a nightclub. I had swung at a guy whose face I could scarcely see in the dark. We'd tripped through the club, clearing the dance floor, knocking over tables, and ended up in a grapple on the floor. Bouncers had pulled us apart and pushed me up against a wall, and a girl had come running over, the nice girl; I couldn't remember her name.

'What happened?' she asked. 'What happened, what happened?'

'I spilt his drink,' I mumbled.

The guy I'd fought with had been watching me. I'd noticed it and not liked it. He had been watching me talk to that nice girl. Then he'd pushed past me in the crowd and his drink spilled.

'Get me a drink,' he'd ordered.

I'd told him to stick his drink. And then it had started.

The bouncers had pinned me against the wall. Everyone stared. The Cloud were appalled – I was not, it seemed, as much like them as I'd wanted to be. I was a loose cannon that had been shot through their mists and was only momentarily falling through their Cloud at some great pace. I liked that nice girl, though. She was kind. Even though I had only been able to make slurred attempts at bland conversation with her, she had smiled, and I momentarily felt like I could sober up into someone less disgusting. I thought perhaps I could find out her name and —

The bouncers pulled me away.

'I didn't start it,' I said.

They understood that, they told me.

They opened a black curtain, and behind it was a red door that they dragged me through and I saw a sign that read: 'Fire Exit'.

'I was defending myself.'

They agreed.

Us three, the bouncers and me, lurched down an echoing concrete stairwell to another fire exit, which they opened onto a dank street.

'Why are you throwing me out?'

'Mate, you have blood all over you. There are no buttons on your shirt, and you are off your face.'

They pushed me into the street. I fell to one knee. I stood and turned and stared at them and they stared back.

'No way,' I said.

They shut the door.

I had been wronged. I wanted to tell the Cloud that I was no different to them. I stood in the street, just off the gutter, breathing deeply.

People were looking at me. I stumbled towards darker spaces.

I don't remember getting home. I remember waking up feeling sick, and tired, and like an outsider. My veneer of cool, that facade, was desperate, a fake load of shit. And people knew it. It made me feel laughably self-conscious. Who was I trying to be that was so awesome?

Who am I?

I had no idea.

Strange anxieties built inside me. A fear of flying that had blinked to life in my mid-twenties became unbearable. On the morning I was to leave for a holiday in the USA, I woke with my muscles already tense from a frightful sleep. I called United Airlines.

'How often do you fly to San Francisco?'

'Once a day, sir.'

'What kind of plane is it?'

'A Boeing 747-400.'

'Right, and do they have two engines?'

'Four engines, sir.'

Shit.

If he'd said only two engines, I wasn't going; 12 000 kilometres over the ocean – stuff that. But the plane had four and that meant I had to go. Four engines meant my fear was irrational. So I went to the airport.

A short time into the flight the captain came over the speakers: 'I've just put the seatbelt sign on. There are a few thunderstorms about, so please keep belted up until we find smooth air.'

It was dark as we zoomed towards foreign time zones. Tiny movie screens bluely illuminated the faces of relaxed passengers.

Below I could sense the ocean, and only air between me and it. I just wanted to sleep and then wake up magically in US airspace. The plane began to lurch and shake. I gripped the armrests, my heart rate increasing, and I was sweating and tense. I got to breaking point.

My God, I can't face this.

There were teenagers, a brother and sister, sitting next to me. They tried to talk to me but I couldn't respond. They read paperback novels, their books jerking from side to side as the plane shuddered.

How are they so calm?

Flight attendants came along the aisle with a drinks cart.

Why are they handing out drinks in an emergency?

'Sir, anything to drink?'

I gave one partially frozen shake of my head.

The siblings ordered Pepsi. I was in the aisle seat, the drink cart bumping my shoulder, and the flight attendant reached across me with Pepsi slapping up against the side of the cup.

Oh, for the love of God.

I began tapping my face, a relaxation technique Dad had shown me.

Even though I have this irrational fear, I do accept myself.

For short moments the air smoothed, and I slid down in my seat and stretched my legs out, one sweaty bastard, but I was never quite able to calm down entirely before tensing again at the prospect of further turbulence. I hoped my parents would get the things I owned if I died. I had some savings, and a car that was 60 per cent owned by a bank, I hoped my parents would get that. On a ticket stub I scribbled a reminder to myself to organise a last will and testament. I didn't sleep. On the descent into San Francisco, my eyes were as big as poker chips.

At the airport I looked at the note on my ticket stub, but all I'd written was: *You make you happy.*

And it made *no* sense. It wasn't even my line; it was something my mother had said to me once, and it was something that I'd never understood.

I spent six weeks in the USA, drinking, clubbing, sleeping in cheap motels until midday. On the flight back to Sydney I could feel the drone of my existence weighing on me as the Australian coastline approached, and I dreaded the life to which I was returning.

DAY
MINUS
1447

I turned thirty.

Somewhere else, probably about 2000 kilometres south-west of Sydney, a great white shark was born. Scientists say that whites are born off South Australia in the Great Australian Bight. They don't know that for sure. I mean, they haven't seen them give birth. But they have found very small and very large great whites together there, and that has not happened elsewhere.

But, anyway, this shark was born, alright – about 1.3 metres long and weighing around 30 kilograms. A decent chunk of fish right off the bat. It was likely born as one of a litter, and would have started to swim up along the Victorian and New South Wales coastlines.

The size of the great white (also known as the white pointer, or white death) is the subject of folklore. I mean, that mother in *Jaws* was big. The largest whites grow to 6 metres in length, with 7-metre individuals reported but not scientifically verified. A 6-metre white weighs approximately 3000 kilograms, and these big ones have a life expectancy of up to sixty years. They have a low natural mortality, as not many other animals can kill a white – well, humans aside. Humans are the whites' greatest threat.

Commercial fishing nets catch great whites as 'bycatch'. The world has tried to stop that. Great whites are now protected in some countries. In 1998, the Australian government recognised a decline in numbers – a reported drop of 60–95 per cent in fifty years – and the great white was protected in Australian waters. In 2004, the international community listed the white as a protected species in the Convention on International Trade in Endangered Species of Wild Fauna and Flora, in an attempt to stop the trade in its teeth, jaws and fins. The jaws of a white can sell for $25 000 and a single tooth can go for $500, and shark fins, for shark fin soup, sell for $130 a kilogram. Fin hunters cut the dorsal and pectoral fins off sharks and throw the sharks back into the water, alive or dead. If they survive the finning, they drown.

But despite the human threat, a great white shark that was born in February 2005 survived, and got busy growing.

DAY
MINUS
1200

I bought an apartment in Cremorne, near the CBD. I moved in with a second-hand microwave, a new fridge and a mattress on the floor. I spent time alone and perpetuating my aloneness. Days rolled into each other: wake up, coffee, fifteen-minute bus ride, work, eat a chicken schnitzel sandwich, work, finish work, walk to the bus stop, arrive home.

Open the fridge. Empty. Open the freezer. Heat up frozen curry. Watch TV.

Nothing.

Stare in the mirror.

Nothing there.

Do sit-ups. Stare at the mirror.

My sleeping was not peaceful; it arrived in a loose collection of overlapping dreams, some new, some remembered.

In my sleep I heard myself speak and the tone of my voice, so fearful, got my attention. But when I woke I'd stopped talking, and I thought that perhaps I'd just been dreaming of speaking in my sleep.

I haven't done anything bad.

It was 5 a.m. I rolled to a sitting position, the carpet under my feet comforting.

What have I done?

No sordid break-ups. No regrets. I hadn't screwed anyone over.

I sat there awake in my quiet, sparsely furnished bedroom and stared up and was just able to make out the immobile ceiling fan in the dark. What I'd been dreaming of came to me: I'd been speaking to Tim, I'd been begging him, *Are you okay? You're going to be okay.*

The Ridgeway crash ran itself through my memory. I threw the blankets off the bed.

Why is this bothering me?

I ran my hand through my hair.

Christ. I'm going bald.

I was exhausted, but anxiety cancels out tiredness and not the other way around. I looked through the window for a long time as the sky turned lead-grey and the shadows over the garden began to lift. I couldn't eat breakfast; there was no food, just beer and frozen pizza. I couldn't go for a run; it was early, and too cold, and my body was stiff and lethargic. I watched the sun lighten the heavy clouds and saw the trees take shape.

What is wrong?

The question frustrated me so much.

My Cremorne apartment was only ever lightly furnished. I had wanted to fit it out more fully, but apathy took over. There was an LCD TV on top of a wood-veneer-type cabinet; a fake thorny plant; a beige shag-pile rug which cost $1000 and which I, soon after purchase, rolled up and hid, in all its hideousness; and a three-seater chocolate-brown sofa that I could just fit on, head to toe.

I spent hours darkly daydreaming on that sofa, and I became obsessed with my health. It so occupied me that I couldn't read, or watch TV, or relax. I could only attempt to rationalise and to curse my irrationality.

It had started with a vist to a doctor. My vision had started to shake and he thought I might have a vitamin deficiency.

'You need a blood test,' he said. 'Are you sexually active?'

'Um . . . Yeah.'

'Well, let's do an STI screen then.'

'Why?'

'Just a precaution.'

Something huge raced up from my subconscious.

What if you have something, you idiot?

I'd not been smart, you know, about safe sex. I'd been an idiot. I thought that if I had caught something, then my whole life would be so shameful to me, and I'd be disgusted in myself – everything would go bad. And I deserved something bad. I hadn't been great. I'd slept with random girls to satisfy my ego and I deserved something bad. That made a lot of sense.

'Here is a lab request.'

The doctor gave me a slip.

I didn't go to the lab, though. I ignored the lab request. Fuck that. But the threat of it wore on me. It ate at my writhing guts and became something that consumed every moment. I spent hours looking up diseases that you can have without knowing. It was a compulsion and the internet can be a curse. After a while I felt I needed to go somewhere I could get away from the fears, but there was no getting away, because I was trapped in my fucking head. I called my mother.

'Hi, darling,' she said.

'Mum, have you ever had panic attacks?'

I heard her exhale, and it was sadness, eyes-closed sadness.

'Yes, honey.'

Mum taught me some breathing techniques and they calmed

me, but my mind did not let up. It stung me at every moment. I took some time off work and went up to the Coast. I sat on my parents' lounge in a state of shock, with a lump in my throat that felt like a golf ball. I pushed at it with my thumb, but it came back tighter.

'It's anxiety,' Mum said.

I shook my head.

'That's not it.'

'You're anxious. You are tensing every muscle in your body. Look at you. The muscles in your throat are spasming – that's what happens with anxiety. You're getting carried away with *thinking*. Whatever you have done, you've blown it out of proportion. You know that. You need to let these thoughts go. Let them just pass through your mind.'

'It's not the thoughts that are the problem,' I snapped. 'It's the problem that's the problem. If I'm sick, then my life is over.'

'You're not sick. The doctor said not to worry.'

'There's a chance I could be.'

'There's a chance you could be hit by a bus.'

'This is different.'

'Glenn. I know this. I've been through anxiety. This is some-thing you're going to have to face up to and learn to deal with.'

Mum suggested I exercise. So I ran. I ran until I could taste blood in my throat. I told myself, *I will not worry about irrational problems.*

Then I went back to Sydney and had the damn tests after all. And there was nothing wrong with me.

'You just need a B12 shot,' the doctor said.

I was elated, delivered. Not evil. Nothing bad like an STI. For two days I felt great. Then the lump came back in my throat and I was perplexed, because nothing was wrong.

Something had started in me that I couldn't stop, some cycle. And soon enough, I had convinced myself that I had cancer of a form with no symptoms but which would disfigure me. It was stupid. And I tried again to rationalise these thoughts away, but an element of me kept it up.

There is a chance, and you deserve it.

What gave these obsessions backbone was the humiliation I felt. It seemed so weak to me that I was unbalanced in some kind of depressive way – fantasising about my own death, unable to let go of what were clearly irrational thoughts. I was a hypochondriac, and I was truly ashamed of myself. I didn't want anyone to know. I strongly believed that I needed to keep silent and make sure no one knew I was so unhappy. So I persevered with these unrelenting obsessions that tempered my happiness and found their voice in all my moments of quiet.

I told myself, *Get over this, you idiot.*

And every night, under a blank ceiling, in an empty bedroom, I spent time tapping on my face.

I will not have irrational fears.

Stu was a friend of other friends who I'd slowly become closer to. He was successful in the construction industry, and was also constructive and practical by nature. He lived a bachelor life like me, but unlike me he always had food in his fridge. He was content and reliable, and willing to listen to my rants about hot chicks and nightclub queues and high society, but really only humoured these forays into bitterness and didn't take them at all seriously. I'd try to goad him into cynicism and sometimes felt like I might be succeeding, but it always dissipated before approaching a critical mass and turned into laughter.

'Come on, mate, you fucken wowser,' he'd say.

In October 2005, Stu and I and some other friends went on holiday to Byron Bay. Byron was just short of its summer pinnacle, with a gathering hustle in the town. Warm weather was swamping everything, and the sea was clear and tepid. We spent the nights drinking, and during the days I stretched out on a pilled couch and read books in the warm, humid hotel room, with towels and clothes hung over every conceivable chair, railing and sill. On the last night there, I was happy, my attention taken by the world and held outside myself for a while. I felt myself relax.

The next morning Stu and I drove back to Brisbane Airport. Just as we left the boundaries of Byron Bay, Stu said, 'Mate, I've got some news.'

'Yeah?'

'I've got cancer.'

I was on the freeway doing 100 kilometres an hour. My foot came off the pedal. I looked him in the face.

'Oh, God. Mate. I am so sorry . . . What do you mean . . . ?'

'Well, I've had this lump in my neck for a while. I didn't know what it was. The doctor said it's stage five lymphoma. He gave me an MRI and it lit up like a Christmas tree.'

'When did you find out?'

'The day before we came. I haven't told anyone yet, just my sister and my dad.'

'Shit. You didn't say *anything*. Why'd you come?'

'I didn't want to spoil the holiday. It was my last hurrah. I've got to stop drinking now, and start eating healthy. I wanted to have this holiday before that.'

I was unable to think of any words. The first thing that came out was, 'I don't know what to say.'

'I know,' he said.

'Is there anything I can do . . . ?'

'Thanks, mate. I'm feeling pretty good about it. The doctor reckons I have a good chance of survival.'

Stu was going to have chemotherapy and possibly a bone

marrow transplant. His attitude was positive, even nonchalant, which was unbelievable to me. I didn't get it. I thought he'd be petrified. But he was calm and refused to entertain hypothetical futures.

'There are some things I can't do anything about,' he'd say.

And he didn't worry about those things. It was an ability he had.

Stu changed his lifestyle. No drinking. Quiet times. He lived alone. His family were not nearby. He was in a fight, and mostly on his own, and there was not a lot anyone could do to edge their way into the fray and get into the fighting too. He didn't talk about his cancer often, preferring only to answer questions if they were asked. He was relying on himself in some kind of rock-solid way that didn't need me unbalancing it. But, to clear the air, I did say, 'I don't like asking you about it. It's hard to know if I should ask or not.'

'Nah, it's fine,' he'd reply. 'Ask me whatever you like. I feel positive about it.'

Stu kept that attitude right through his chemo: positive and optimistic. In life-threatening circumstances he proved his true character. He had a gracious and rare grit, and I felt small against him in comparison, small against his dignity. His problems made my problems nothing. My health obsessions were merely a mental abstraction. I pandered to irrational fears, while Stu had real fear to deal with and was dealing with it like a man.

I decided I had to do one good thing that wasn't about me. I had good blood – I knew this from all the tests I'd had – and so I gave blood. With the needle in my arm, I kept thinking positive thoughts.

This will save a life. Feel good about it.

DAY
MINUS
800

Mud was getting married and he asked me to be his best man. Some previously long-gone feeling ran along my jaw, down my throat and behind my eyes – pride, relief? Had I done something right? If he'd asked me to do this, then I couldn't have been so bad.

We had always been close, Mud and I, right since those first days when we met at the uni rugby club. We'd been flatmates, played in sports teams together, and his wife-to-be, Ness, and I were friends. The night I'd broken up with Elizabeth, I had crashed at Mud's place, because it had felt like the easiest, most right thing to do.

However, since I'd been single I'd drifted away from him. I'd wanted to go to loud, brash bars and drink fifteen vodkas and get hyper and have the best night ever, and meet chicks. Mostly that. I went out to escape, for a moment, from an average life. I was sure it looked pathetic, rabid and kind of dirty, and so had started to avoid my good friends. That's how crazy I was getting. So Mud asking me to be his best man came out of the blue; he could have easily asked someone else, and that would have been upsetting, but, damn it, he asked me. I was excited. It came at a low point in my life and was an immediate reality check, a grounding. No matter how bad

I felt, I had this friendship that was much truer than the nonsense of my daily existence and it was a solid pillar to find my feet on.

I had been reading a book about healthy self-talk, and subsequently had started telling myself:

I am healthy. I am compassionate. I am valuable.

But my mind had rebutted those axioms with criticism:

I am sick, useless and boring – to everyone.

The self-talk book had predicted this would happen, and I was supposed to respond with more calming self-talk, which, for me, only resulted in a fiery internal debate.

I'm the best man, though.

That statement caused silence in my head. There was no retort. It was a fact. Mud had confidence in my worth as a person – I had that. The day I was Mud's best man was a high honour in my life.

Around that same time, in February 2006, somewhere in the expanse, on an east-coast voyage, the great white shark turned one year old. It was stocky with a stout, torpedo-shaped body. Above the water its grey dorsal fin was almost an equilateral triangle, and underneath it was all white. Now about 1.6 metres long, it had grown 20 per cent in one year, and it had thickened as well, weighing now close to 50 kilograms. An impressive animal, the shark had several rows of continually growing teeth, warm blood, great vision, a sense of smell far superior to ours, and a line of nerves along its body that could sense vibrations in the water. And the great white had its ampullae of Lorenzini – little gel-filled sacks in the snout that pick up the electrical signals associated with the muscle movements of its prey. I mean, how many senses does it need? The white outmatches nearly everything in the ocean.

Sometimes the great white cruises with other whites. It's a social thing. Scientists have witnessed coordinated pack hunting in great white sharks. And one other thing is clear to those scientists: whites are intelligent. And that makes sense, because they prey on large-brained, social animals like seals and dolphins and need to be intelligent to outwit their prey.

This one-year-old great white was not yet big enough to eat seals; it fed on finfish and smaller sharks. It began to follow a well-worn migration path between Victoria and New South Wales.

I walked along the Manly Beach promenade on a Saturday afternoon. It was autumnal, dusk, and a crisp hint of cool air snuck under the remaining sunlight. People strolled along the promenade in couples, or with dogs, and joggers weaved through. I had the hood of my jumper over my head, my shadow merging with the shadows of palms trees on the pavement, then reappearing, then disappearing. I went by a surf shop and was drawn into it by the boards in the window, the smooth longboards. I slid my hand along the pristine rails, and pulled them out of the rack to look at their shape. It had been years since I had paid attention. Touching them brought back memories of walking out of the surf on a cold afternoon: stripping off a wetsuit in the car park, the chill air, wrapping up in warm clothes.

In the surf shop, a guy with fuzzy black hair and a foreign accent approached me while I ran my hand along the rail of a board.

'Can I help you?' he asked.

I shook my head. 'Just looking.'

I stepped along. The next board was a second-hand longboard, the wax on the deck in a perfect pattern of white lumps. I looked at the stringer and the label said it was 8 feet long. The board was thin and had curve, and it had a bright orange stripe down its deck. I knew I wanted it, and I don't even like bright orange.

'That's a McTavish Carver,' the guy said.

'It says "high performance"?'

'Yep. It's a bit thinner, really fast and light. Here, feel it.'

He handed it to me.

Hmm, high performance.

'It's really good for carving and cruising,' he added.

Hmm, carving and cruising.

I walked out of the shop with that $700, second-hand, 8-foot, orange-striped McTavish, and it only just fit in the car.

I'll come home from surfing so tired that I'll just go right to sleep, and have no dreams . . . Something in my life.

I plonked the longboard in the corner of my bedroom. It looked good. I didn't use it.

Late in 2006, I sat in a bar alone. Stu was sick. His legs were swelling; he was starting to look sick. Soon he'd be in hospital for chemo. I drank alone, not wanting to go home, not wanting to think about what Stu had to think about. I went to the bar to look at people. I checked my hair a few times, each time taking a second of comfort because it looked acceptable, and each moment after that wishing I wasn't the type of person to draw comfort from that. I tucked my shirt in and buttoned up my suit. It was Friday night. The bar was packed. The air-conditioning was on. The marquee of a room with high ceilings and a marble floor was loud with chatter and clinking. Next to me was an old guy in a suit with very good hair. I hoped I wouldn't be seen by anyone I knew. I didn't want to be seen alone. I fooled around with my mobile phone.

Why am I here?

All across the bar were men in suits laughing in the dark. I was indiscernible, indistinguishable; just another guy in a grey suit.

DAY
MINUS
770

I know what the most important moment of my life has been, and it has nothing to do with sharks. When this moment occurred, I didn't realise its significance straightaway; on the scale of all moments, it seemed like only a rather good moment, a satisfying slice of life that would leave a happy memory. I didn't see it as a turning point. I didn't realise how much love, honesty, contentment, passion and hard work it would bring me. Without this moment, I never would have survived the shark attack.

At noon on 30 December 2006, I drove to the Peats Ridge Music Festival north of Sydney. My siblings, Tim, Sarah and Richard, had insisted that I go with them, but I was sceptical.

On the one hand, I wanted to spend time with my siblings, and my niece, Mika, and to see Tim's band, which was playing at the festival. And I had a nagging voice telling me that I needed to try something different, a voice that said staying in Sydney for New Year's Eve would result in the same hangover, the same disappointment, the same feeling of fatness and laziness that I had awoken with on the previous five New Year's Days. On the other hand (and it is painful to be honest about this now), the single man in me wanted to meet women, wanted to pick up, wanted action, and a hippy music festival out in the sticks seemed a poor option for those purposes.

Saturday 30 December was a warm day. It took an hour to wind down the dirt road into the Glenworth Valley with the other vehicles. The crowd was building. I pitched a tent as the music was starting and then I was unsure of what to do. I decided to give the festival until early evening, and if it was shit I'd leave.

I sat down in a shanty called the Love Shack, and, at a loss, with flummoxing menu options, I ordered a tofu burger. A lot of the people walking around the festival wore loose Thai fishermen pants. A man with dreadlocks down to his waist walked past with his shirt off; whippet-thin, darkly tanned, with curls of hair shooting off his chest, he was stoned into orbit. I was wearing a tight, button-up, collared, long-sleeve business shirt and cargo shorts. Damn, I was out of place. Long grass reached over my thongs, my hair was sticky and flat, the shirt was too tight.

I noticed a few people at a nearby table. One of them was Lisa.

We smiled at each other.

It was that. That was the moment.

I hadn't meant to catch her eye. I mean, I was looking in her direction, not staring, just, you know, browsing. And then our eyes connected. Her smile had a genuine, friendly quality. I felt at ease just looking at her, and I did not generally feel at ease. She was beautiful. She was wearing a summer hat, and under it was her long straight auburn hair, and she had noticeably smooth skin, and I'm just a big sucker for that kind of skin. She was stunning.

Natural, I thought instantly.

Later, I wondered about that thought, *natural*, trying to figure out what the hell I meant by it. Did I mean confident? I know now that there is nothing inside her that is off-limits to her, that she can face the giants on the inside: sadness, regret, happiness and humiliation.

Face them, not just endure them – confront them right there, burning in whatever manner they will.

She smiled, and I – unsure that it was even aimed at me, and feeling that I might need to check behind me – just spontaneously returned it. It was the first smile of mine in a long time that felt real. She took off her sunglasses, and her eyes came out all big and perfect. Things happened quickly. I never got a chance to turn to plastic.

She got up from her table and walked towards the drink fridge in the Love Shack, which was near where I was sitting. I tried not to look at her, and I just flicked the tofu burger ticket between my fingers. But at the last moment I looked into her eyes and said 'Hi' as she passed.

'Hi,' she said.

The sun was on my back, there was a thickness in the air, and tofu was hissing on a barbecue somewhere.

What will I say when she comes back? 'Hi'? Again? She's just being friendly. It's the vibe. It's festive. I just don't have any—

Lisa sat down next to me.

'Hi,' I said again.

We fell into an engaging conversation, and I was taken away as if I'd been standing in a speedboat that had just accelerated and caused me to fall into the seat. There was a whirlwind of openness. I was answering searching questions without qualm, and my noticing this lack of qualm had me on the edge of a nervous chortle. Lisa was entirely calm. I attempted charm and honesty (and, admittedly, also slight indifference). I thought we were flirting and she liked me. I was thinking that she was liking me, and, really, I was liking her.

She's flirting, right? This is flirting.

I told her I was thinking of leaving the festival, and instead of asking why she said, 'Me, too.'

Her grandfather had passed away during the night. I shied away from that topic, not wanting to intrude, feeling awkward, uncomfortable with her grief.

Lisa's memory of our conversation is that I was cold and guarded, though she could tell that I liked her. She wasn't sure if she liked me. She had surprised herself, greatly, by sitting down to talk to me; she can't explain why she did that. She felt that I was distracted and she imagined (my choice of word, because this part is not correct) that I was checking out other girls. She thought I was hiding something and she recalls catching only glimmers of a real person beneath a clumsy bravado.

I ate the tofu burger and then I walked with Lisa and her friends around the festival. We ran into my two-year-old niece, Mika, a beautiful, cheeky little thing at home in the community atmosphere of the festival and its dusty paddocks. I chased her around Tim's tent and she hid under an A-frame sign. She jumped out to scare me with her little hands in tiny claws. I played along, but after a while I told Mika that I was going to have to leave.

'No,' she said.

'We'll play later,' I told her.

'No.'

'Bye, Mika.'

I tried to kiss her, but she ducked away and hid under the sign, and from there said, 'I love you.'

She had never said that to me before. I dropped onto a knee, and gave her a peck on the cheek.

'I love you, too,' I told her.

In seeing me with Mika, Lisa thought she'd seen the real me, and she decided to stay at the festival.

Lisa and I spent the afternoon together. Her friends were there, and I was aware that I was totally crashing their party, but the humiliation was mild because it was worth it. We watched bands that I didn't know the names of. We sat in circus tents, and I was even cajoled into dancing to hillbilly rock.

In the evening, as it cooled off and the crowd grew, we started drinking. I relaxed into my comfort zone of alcohol confidence. A touch of inhibition lost, a forgetting of the vanity, a feeling that I'm funny. We drank sangria, and toasted with it, and I said some inane things which were so mindless that Lisa teased me about them, but which have since become meaningful because they're part of our story now.

At midnight we found two plastic chairs in the middle of a huge crowd where no other chairs existed. We sat down and joked around, and we kissed. At 2 a.m. we drank chai tea in a tent full of sleeping hippies and then I walked Lisa back to her camp. We held hands and through a balmy stillness we weaved around grassy hills. At her campsite she slipped away into darkness. I walked to my tent, and lay awake watching the stars shine through the green mesh.

Lisa and I had arranged to meet the next morning at the Love Shack. At 9 o'clock, in a limp crowd, I stood waiting. She was nowhere, and I had a half-hour of my confidence wavering before she arrived at 9.30.

'You're late,' she said.

'No, I'm not.'

'A little joke. Look,' she said, holding up her phone to me. 'It's dead.'

'That's no good.'

I kissed her hello, shy but candid, and kind of self-conscious in the crowd of strangers. We had breakfast together and talked, a little awkwardly. But as the day went on we relaxed, and later, in a surreal open-mic tent, while sitting on flattened grass, she leaned into me and my arm went round her, and her hair, bulky and soft, pressed against my cheek. I felt that a cuddle was a far greater act of affection than our situation warranted, and yet I just really fucking loved it.

In the afternoon she asked me, 'Are you okay?'

I was pale.

'I'm okay,' I said.

It was 3 p.m. She left then, with her friends, and we agreed to meet up again at 6 to watch Tim's band play.

I did laps of the festival with Richard. It was hot, dry and dusty. I felt parched and got some water. As soon as I sipped it I thought, *Uh-oh.*

The water went down my gullet all scratchy and unrefreshing, just like the chai tea had gone down the night before.

'I'm getting a cold,' I said to Richard.

'Aw, bullshit. You'll be right.'

'It's from that fucking chai tent,' I said.

Richard and I rambled around the festival, drinking brown bottled beer, weaving through long-haired crowds. I got a headache. Around 6 we arrived at the tent Tim was playing in. His band started and the whole tent began dancing. Dust flew up, creating a knee-high cloud. It further dried my dry throat. I watched Mika dancing in a cloud of dust that covered her.

By 6.30, Lisa still hadn't showed. I stood to the side of the tent, at an airway at the edge of the crowd. My head was thumping. The beer tasted horrible.

If she doesn't turn up, it will be depressing.

I surveyed the crowd.

Maybe she went to the wrong tent? Maybe she's in another crowd, standing on tiptoe, looking at a sea of heads. Maybe I should go and look for her.

The dust, the music, the crowd: it suffocated me. It pushed me out of the tent and into the long stringy grass. I sat down. I swallowed and my Adam's apple passed over a cheese grater.

I'm sick.

I poured my beer onto the grass. Richard asked me if I was okay. My headache was hateful. My throat urged me away. I croaked that I was sick and trudged off to my tent, then stripped to my undies and lay, splayed, on my blow-up mattress, listening to the shouts and muffled music.

I took a Panadol and my headache got worse. I took two more Panadols, right away, in order to stop the feelings emanating from my body, and that quelled them a little, but my throat felt awful.

It got dark. The party went wild. I just lay there, for hours. The green mesh of the tent became steamy and unpleasant. I lay awake. My phone beeped a few times – messages from friends and my brothers and sister wondering where the hell I was. Nothing from Lisa. At one point Tim and his wife, Aimie, and Mika came to visit me.

'You okay, bro?'

By then it was hard to speak.

'I feel terrible.'

'Can we do anything?'

'No.'

'We miss you,' said Aimie.

'We miss you,' echoed Mika.

They sang a get-well chant they knew.

Richard came and unzipped my tent and rushed in on top of me.

'Mate, what are you doing, cockhead?' he said.

I groaned.

'Oh, you're sick. That's a shocker.'

'Is it good?'

'The festival? It's awesome. '

'Did you see Lisa?'

'Nah, man.'

Lisa had moved from drinking sangria to absinthe, but by 11 p.m. she was sobering up. She felt bad about standing me up. The plan had always been for her to spend the New Year with her friends, and she'd felt torn between them and me. She had wanted to cancel our meeting, but her phone was busted. She'd hoped she would run into me at the festival somewhere, somehow, just by chance, because she was a romantic at heart. But I was in the tent.

Lisa grew tired, and increasingly sad about her grandfather, and she missed me and felt weird, because she felt so strongly about that. When it was late, past midnight, she sadly walked back through the drunkenness to her tent. She thought about going past my tent, but worried that I might've had another girl in there.

All night I rolled over and over on my stinking air mattress until the festival quietened and footsteps began to stumble past my tent. When the green mesh was illuminated by yellow dawn, I left the festival and drove to my parents' place, which was close by. My throat spat flames onto the roof of my mouth and I dribbled into fifty different tissues. I got a fever and sweated profusely.

Dad, who's a doctor, opened my mouth so he could look in, and it was like opening a rusty gate.

'Come on, mate. Open up,' he said.

You open up, I wanted to say, but it came out, 'Ooo ohen ahhhhr.'

He pulled my mouth open and I shut my eyes; it was unbearable. I had tonsillitis, close to being quinsy. He handed me pills, antibiotics and strong painkillers. I gave him a quizzical look.

I wasn't putting any pills into the tiny gap I had for a gullet. I pointed at my throat.

'See if you can get it down, mate,' he said. 'Otherwise I'll have to take you to hospital for a shot.'

I slipped the pill in between my lips, and the swallowing was torture.

Sometime after that, I got a message from Lisa.

Whatever.

I didn't read it. I planned never to read it, but its bleeping head-line ('Lisa', 'Lisa') was not easy to ignore, and the more it called for my attention the less righteous I felt. In fact, I was relieved that she'd sent a message – it meant she had thought about me. I told myself that she must've had a good reason to stand me up, something una-voidable.

Lisa already meant something to me, I felt we had a connection, and this was a feeling that was much more insistent than it ought to have been. I wanted to believe she was feeling it too. I finally got some sleep anyway.

A few days into January, Lisa and I spoke on the phone. We talked about the stand-up. Her reasons seemed clear, but this didn't really relieve my disappointment. She apologised and I decided I would just accept it. I was acting on instinct and managed to get over the incident when normally it would have snared me. Something stopped me from just quitting. I really wanted to see her again.

On the night of our first date, it was warm, and it was daylight saving and the sun was still out for an hour before it would set. Lisa's lived in Bondi, on a leafy and cluttered street, and I could smell bar-becue and ocean. I was wearing tan shoes, blue jeans and a white collared shirt. As I walked up the concrete steps of her apartment complex, I had the sudden feeling that I didn't really know her.

I mean, I knew who she was, and I knew what she looked like, but the details of her face were vague to me. Maybe everything between us had just been a brief romance.

She opened the door smiling, and straightaway I recalled her smile. Her hair was curly, different to how I remembered. She wore brown thongs, tight black jeans and a black singlet. And I realised that I had been wrong, because I did know her. And there was something between me and this beautiful girl.

'You look dressy,' she said. 'I'm just wearing thongs.'

That's how it started: me trying to be impressive, her seeing right through it.

DAY MINUS 717

Lisa showed me Bondi. She'd lived there her whole life and was enchanted by it. Before seeing Bondi through Lisa's eyes, I'd thought the eastern suburbs were pretentious. Bondi, and haunts close by, have posh aspects to their character: exclusive nightclubs where queues stretch down the block, beautiful people, expensive restaurants, silicon and social pages, tourist traps, and Real Estate. And I, having previously focused on superficial pleasures, had only ever seen in Bondi the brash action that flocked into and out of spilling bars. But beyond those shallow antics it had a backbone, a community. I had no concept of neighbours that became friends, or shopkeepers who remembered their customers' names; things like that hadn't existed in places I had lived, and it was a surprise to find them in Bondi. In reality, once I looked, there was a real mix of people: the locals and the hippies, and travellers and revellers, the A, B and Z list, and surfers. Not much looked unusual in Bondi, and wearing tracksuit pants down the street was actually quite fine and damn liberating. The only problem was finding a car park.

Lisa said, 'You only bought that Jeep because you think it makes you look cool, didn't you?'

'No,' I said. 'Nup, I bought a Jeep because I need the room for my surfboard.'

'Oh, that's such rubbish. You bought it because you think it's cool.'

'No. I mean —'

'Don't worry.' She grabbed my arm and put it around her. 'I won't tell anyone.'

On Valentine's Day 2007, Lisa came to my apartment for dinner. She was upset. Unexpectedly she'd received a present from her ex-boyfriend of chocolates and pillows embroidered with 'I love you'. That kind of vociferous sentimentality was a shock to her and freaked her out. I told her not to worry and she didn't talk much more about it, but she was distant and obviously distracted. I wanted her to forget it, but she couldn't. It started a tension that became a halting argument that neither one of us wanted but which gained momentum anyway. Dinner was abandoned.

'Do you want me to go?' she asked.

'Yeah, you should,' I said

We stood in the hallway, near the front door. I tensed, ready for her to walk out. I wanted her to stay, but I wasn't going to say a word. If she wanted to end it there, it would end. I didn't have the communication skills to pull it back from the brink, and I would remain silent despite the pain. She looked at me.

'I have always done this,' she said. 'Walked out. It's not who I want to be any more.'

She took a step towards me.

'Let's not do this.'

We sat down, I took a breath and she laughed in a little way that made me crack a smile. I said, 'I've always stormed out, that's been my thing.'

'It doesn't work.'

We both knew what we didn't want, so we got into an agreement not to storm out on each other. It was an important moment. It made us closer. We set up this rule that stopped previous behaviours, made transparent a fault we both had, and underlined our mutual respect.

After that night we were official, exclusive, boyfriend and girlfriend, whatever it's called. Our relationship gathered steam and major milestones raced past before I had the chance to analyse them. Typically I would have jumped off a steam train like that into some single-man abyss, and made everything stop until I could assess the greenness of the grass in some other location. But – I was in love with her, see.

Later that summer, Lisa and I went to the Tropfest short film festival. It was a balmy night, and in the CBD parkland thousands of people sprawled on the grass. Stu came. He was sick, in the middle of chemotherapy, and having to tough out every hour at that stage. It was the first time Lisa had met Stu and they hit it off. Lisa got on so easily with people and could make them laugh. Everyone was sitting on blankets, but Stu was uncomfortable on the ground so Lisa organised a deckchair for him to sit in. A few times that night I noticed both their faces reflecting the sheen from the big screen and laughing.

The next day Stu wrote me an email: 'She's a keeper, mate.'

It meant a lot to me.

Summer moved into early autumn, and Bondi in March is perfect. The crowds are dwindling, backpackers leave to go up the coast, autumn starts to touch the morning, the twilight is still and quiet and lasts forever, the cafes and shops are open late, and from Lisa's apartment I could smell the sea.

On 5 March, Lisa put a photo of me on her fridge. I was the only non-family member on there. I remember that.

The great white turned two years old. Big enough by then, at 1.9 metres long, to take a chunk – but still a juvenile, still small enough to get taken by something bigger as well. Juvenile whites don't live near adult whites, because the big ones prey on smaller ones. So juvenile whites avoid seal colonies, and hang out together in other locations. Juveniles are like that.

In 2007, the CSIRO tagged ten juvenile whites from New South Wales' Stockton Beach. Satellites picked up the signals from the tags as these juveniles moved along the east coast. They were found to reside in several locations: at the north end of Stockton Beach; in Corner Inlet, near Wilsons Promontory in Victoria; and sometimes up towards Fraser Island in Queensland. The data showed a migration pattern: in spring the juveniles migrated from Stockton Beach to Corner Inlet, before returning north in late autumn. On their migration, the sharks rarely stopped in any location for longer than a day. They just swam the 800-kilometre trip, nonstop, and arrived at their destination in eleven to twelve days. So if a juvenile approached any beaches on the way, it was just visiting. Researchers had found that the juveniles along the east coast formed a single, mobile population: those at Stockton Beach were the same ones turning up at Corner Inlet.

The CSIRO data demonstrated that great whites are capable of travelling long distances. In December 2007, a 2.1-metre male left Stockton Beach and turned up in New Zealand at a time well-known for the presence of jack mackerel and gummy sharks; it knew where it was going and why. The scientists weren't sure how it had navigated over such a distance, because it swam to New Zealand in a straight line, over 2000 kilometres. Those juvenile sharks, they're not just swimming around the ocean randomly.

The CSIRO plots their tagging data with little yellow dots on a map. And on their maps, the area around the northern end of Stockton Beach, known as Birubi Point, looks like it's covered with yellow confetti. This would not surprise the locals, as nearby Hawks Nest Beach has often been closed due to shark sightings. There's something going on around Stockton that attracts the juveniles.

Stockton Beach is genuine, rugged Australian coastline. Near there, 200 kilometres from Bondi, a yellow dot on a map marked where a two-year old great white was eating fish and getting bigger.

DAY
MINUS
676

Damo, my mate from uni days, got engaged to Charlotte, and I missed their engagement party. I was in the car, with Lisa, when he called.

'Mate, are you coming to this engagement party?'

'Ah, I forgot to tell you. I've got a dinner thing on.'

'This is my engagement party.'

I looked over at Lisa. I had stuffed up. I'd forgotten about the engagement party, and had promised Lisa I would meet her family at dinner. I was screwed.

Damo had never met Lisa, he didn't know anything about her; I'd been busy for months and hadn't even seen the guy. Basically, I felt like shit – I knew I'd let him down. But I didn't go to his party. I wanted to make a good impression on Lisa's family.

'I'll make it up to you,' I told him.

Damo and I had grown apart over the years of my single life. He'd been in a serious relationship; he liked surfing, rugby and barbecues. While I, in between bouts of surreptitious anxiety, had been sleeping late, drinking late and chasing girls at loud bars. No-showing at his engagement party was clear evidence of my narcissism that was hard for either of us to ignore.

'Everything alright?' Lisa asked me.

'Fine.' I gave a thin smile. 'Fine.'

Soon after, I found out that Damo was having five groomsmen at his wedding, and that I wasn't one of them. It hurt. Perhaps it shouldn't have hurt – possibly I should have expected it, probably I had brought it on myself. But it hurt. I'd found it out second-hand, via an overheard conversation. I wished he had told me.

'Speak to him about it,' said Lisa.

But I was too embarrassed to ask him if I was less than his fifth best friend. I didn't want verbal confirmation of my suspicion that I was on the outer – or, worse, to see surprise on his face that I even considered myself a fifth best friend candidate. I preferred to keep silent, and pretend all was just as expected. But then Damo said he needed to speak to me.

I met him at The Oaks, a pub in Cremorne. He was in the car-peted back bar, sitting at a wooden table, with his beer half sunk. There was a small crowd, a TV playing football. Damo looked nerv-ous, and I felt sorry for him.

'What's up?' I said.

And I was about to say, 'Don't worry about it. I already know, and it's fine. I realise that missing your engagement party was not good, so don't feel bad about not having me in your wedding party, you don't have to apologise or anything.'

But I didn't say that, because Damo started talking.

'Well,' he said, 'of course I've been worrying about this.' He waved his hands abstractedly. 'And, you know, I hate confrontation, but I just don't get you. You're unreliable, and when you are around you're distracted, you only talk about chicks. Like, where the hell is the guy I know?'

There was tension in his face. It took a lot for him to say that, and I agreed with him. I'd lost myself, that was true. (Accidental, but true.) I'd already spoken to Lisa about these things. I didn't know what to say to Damo. I wanted our close friendship back. So I just told him about Lisa, and what she meant to me. I said that I was planning to change a few things. Damo explained his choices for his wedding. He understood that I was disappointed, and I understood his decision.

I left The Oaks feeling better than I had for a long time. I'd been pretty open. I'd been, I guess, real, and things that had gone off track had been left pointing in a better direction. Damo had guts; that conversation was no easy thing.

He and Charlotte ended up inviting Lisa to their wedding, even though they had never met her. That was heartening, I felt good about that. But at the wedding, beautiful though it was, I was also sad because I felt I should have been up there with Damo. Lisa was good, though – she didn't let me go swimming in the sadness.

Lisa liked letters, cards, notes, and she wanted me to write to her.

'Talk from your heart.'

'Huh?'

'*Talk* from your *heart*,' she repeated.

I didn't know what she meant.

I wrote her a few short stories. I thought they were super funny and creative, but they upset her. I wrote her a story about a shark attack that was a veiled metaphor for painful isolation. She thought that was bizarre. I wrote her a short story about a man who contracted gynaecomastia and grew D-cup breasts with dinner plate-sized nipples. She questioned if I was serious about our relationship. She said that writing crazy stories was a bullshit way for me to avoid telling her how I felt. I (naively) told Lisa that a woman had once described me as emotionally barren. Oh, that stuck; Lisa took that as an accurate analysis of my potential, and things got difficult.

'I don't want to go on like this. You have to start opening up to me,' she said.

'What do you mean?'

'You have a front up, a bravado. You hate talking about yourself. You can't tell me how you feel.'

'I feel . . . good.'

'"Good" is not a feeling. Speak from your heart.'

It was babble to me. I wasn't hiding anything, I just didn't know how to open up like she wanted. I reached inside and stirred around, but nothing floated to the surface that was worthy of discussion, only irrational things – anxieties, humiliations. I looked up. She was serious.

'I really am happy, you know,' I said, and I motioned to her, and she knew that I meant her by that.

'But, what?' she asked.

I had to tell her something. I had a moment in which I thought to lie and invent a safe problem that I could pretend to resolve with her.

Life can't go on like this, I thought, *this hiding, this living without risk; it's not a life.*

I looked at her, and into her face, and I said, 'I worry about being sick.'

'What do you mean?'

'That I might have caught something, like, from someone.'

She frowned. 'But you've been tested and you're fine?'

'Yeah, but a while ago I went to a public toilet, and when I went in, there was a man and I think he was a drug addict, and he smelt like piss, but I had to go, so I went into the stall he was leaving, and afterwards realised I had touched everything he had just touched.'

'You can't get anything from that.'

I paused, looking down, and reluctantly I said, 'You can.'

'This bothers you?'

I nodded. 'It's stupid. But there is always something like this in my mind. It haunts me. For a moment I'm happy, and then I remember it and it makes me panic. I hate it. I don't want people to know I worry about this shit.'

I was ashamed of how ridiculous my anxiety was, and disgusted with how pathetic I became in the face of it. She just listened calmly before saying, 'Maybe it's not the problem that's the problem.'

'Huh?'

'Well, this is irrational.'

'It's totally irrational, but knowing that doesn't make it go away. Actually, if anything, it makes it —'

'No, but maybe this health anxiety is a symptom of something else, underneath it, that is going on for you. Some fear, or something that you haven't dealt with that is now coming out in this way.'

'I'm sorry,' I said, 'that just sounds like mumbo jumbo.'

'The one thing I know is that if you resist a feeling, it will get stronger, and it will come out somehow.'

I broke eye contact, and stared at the wall. Mum had said something like that to me once as well. I didn't like it. Our conversation was going down an intense path, and I hated intense discussions. I really did not want to be there, on a quiet night, having a crap discussion about something that had proved to be uncontrollable, that no one really knew anything about except me. I was getting angry.

'Why are you getting angry?' she asked.

'I'm not.'

'Maybe what I am saying is right?'

'Righto. Sure.'

I got up and walked into the kitchen. She followed. She put her arms around my middle.

'I'm just trying to help you.'

'Yeah, well, this doesn't help, okay? This kind of conversation does not help.'

'You know,' she said, and paused. 'You could go and see someone, a therapist —'

'Oh, please!' I unwrapped her arms and pushed my fingers into
my eyes. 'Please don't start with that. I'm not doing that, and I will
never do it. It's not me.'

That ended the discussion. I just wanted to see a doctor, a medical doctor, and get another test for some peace of mind. If a doctor
told me that I was being irrational, I would feel better for a while.
But Lisa insisted that I shouldn't go to the doctor.

'That's the opposite of what you need to do. That will solve your
problem for two seconds and then the next thing will come along.
The next drama will send you spinning off into paranoia land. You
need to sit with this feeling, Glenn. It's telling you something.'

She seemed so sure of this, and she said to me, 'You are a good
person, Glenn. I know that. But you need to know that too.'

It meant so much to me when she said this, because despite what
I'd told her, she hadn't changed her view of me. She believed in her
view of me, and in this view I was loved. That changed my life.

For Easter 2007, Lisa and I went to the Byron Bay Blues and Roots
music festival with some friends. On the third night, Jack Johnson
made a surprise appearance in the acoustic tent, and that put us
on a high. Outside the tent, in the dark, Lisa and I stood in each
other's arms. A crowd streamed past us. The rain had stopped for
a moment, and the clouds parted just enough for us to see the moon.

'I love the moon,' she said.

'Me, too,' I said.

We had been going out for three months. I asked her to marry
me. The proposal came out in a rush, and what I heard myself say
sounded very right.

DAY
MINUS
640

I moved in to Lisa's Bondi apartment. She had made that apartment a home, and it became mine too. I loved waking up to the smell of the ocean. Lisa made me get up early; she wanted to go walking, or get coffee, or go swimming. I wanted to sleep, but Lisa insisted on 6 a.m. starts, and she was persuasive or persistent, or both. She would spread her arms out at the vista of the sun rising over the sea.

'How lucky are we? Look at where we live!'

We walked past the cafe where my brother Richard had once worked.

'I used to get coffee from your brother,' Lisa said. 'He always looked so angry.'

'Yeah,' I said. 'He's a bit like me.'

'What do you mean?'

I just shrugged. I didn't tell her that I had become aware of an inexplicable anger that took me over on bus rides, and in the car, and walking to work in the morning. It was an anger that I had thought was gone, something I remembered from my youth, which had come back razor-edged. It was as if it had only been pushed to the side of my brain and ignored, somehow, but had never truly gone. Each morning I caught myself, teeth gritted, daydreaming of fistfights or arguments. I had cracked the enamel on my teeth. My dentist told me to stop grinding or I'd have to wear a plate, so I forced myself to notice when I was clenching my teeth in anger. Previously I'd been unconscious of the habit, unaware that I had surrendered to it, that it had taken me over, and I'd arrive at work with anger full up inside me and hanging over my head. It was weird to find such a severe reaction going on that I'd been blind to before.

Lisa went to ask another question, but dropped it before it got to her lips. She smiled instead, and I put my arm around her as we walked.

I came to like those early morning walks: the quietness, the cool, the lack of crowds. I noticed surfers running past me, and I noticed the waves. I would dawdle along the promenade watching the ocean. Lisa saw what I was staring at. She asked me why I'd stopped surfing.

'You stopped because you had a fight with Luke?'

'Well, it's more complicated than that . . .'

'So, that's a yes?'

'No —'

'It sounds like yes.'

'I started playing rugby. None of my mates at uni surfed. Surfing just got stale, somehow, the pleasure . . .'

'So why do you always stand here and stare at the waves like a nebbish?'

'Pardon?'

'Can you even surf?'

'Yes, I can, actually.'

'Well, don't take out that big mal when you're around me, because it's embarrassing.'

She was talking about my 8-foot McTavish.

'It's actually quite a good board. It's high performance.'

'It's an old man's board.'

'Okay.'

'You're an old man.'

'Okay.'

'You can't even surf, anyway.'

'Righto, off you go.'

Lisa strode off, power-walking and laughing along the promenade, and I walked over to the rail to lean against it and watch the waves.

Bondi Beach is interesting, from a surfing perspective. You see, it faces south-east, and a lot of Sydney swell comes from the south. New Zealand and other Pacific Islands stop swell coming from the east. Occasionally a low-pressure system plants itself in the Tasman Sea and then some big easterly swell might arrive, and an occasional tropical cyclone in Queensland might send refracted north-east swell into Sydney. But, mostly, it is Antarctic storms that send up southerly swell onto the New South Wales coast. Bondi picks up every dribble of a south swell. It is good in that way.

But Bondi also has negative attributes. For one thing, it is only 1 kilometre long, and that affects the waves. When the swell gets bigger than, say, head-high, the sandbanks seem to merge into a continuous kilometre-long sandbank, and the waves break over it in a big, unsurfable close-out. The fact is, Bondi is not great in bigger swells.

And another pressing negative attribute is the crowd. Bondi attracts a lot of international visitors – visitors who, understandably, want to sample the splendour of Australia's beaches and the surfing lifestyle. There are several surf schools in Bondi, and when you add the learners to a group of more advanced surfers that have either grown up in the area or have moved to Bondi for a beach lifestyle, you have a recipe for surfing entanglements, occasional arguments and a lot of hassling for waves. Surfing etiquette can be unknown to learners and ignored by advanced surfers, and every breaking wave can be a shitfight of people crossing over each other, dinging each other's boards, yelling and causing occasional bodily harm.

And if a day of clean 2-foot waves occurs on a 30-degree weekend in the middle of summer, with visitors from all over Sydney pouring in, various promotions, news choppers and seaplanes flying overhead, the coffee shops overflowing, so many people on the beach that you cannot see the sand, barbecues and parties at the north end, the Sculpture by the Sea, the buses, the southern 'backpacker' rip and a distinct lack of parking – then you have a good excuse to stay in the house all day and just watch the carnage on *Bondi Rescue*.

The crowd in the water had been one of the factors keeping me away from surfing in the city. However, in the very early morning, while the council man was still cleaning up the rubbish left on the sand from the weekend, it was – a little – less crowded. I saw the same guys getting all the good waves out there.

'The thing about Bondi,' said my friend Binnie when we discussed it, 'is that a lot of the learners out there just don't get that many waves. They're out there, but they aren't catching much.'

So I came to the conclusion that the crowd was manageable. I knew it would be frustrating at times, but I sensed that there would also be moments of space. The crowd was a fact, and I decided to accept it. At least it would lower the chances of a shark attack.

So in the mornings, while Lisa went walking, I started running down to the beach with the 8-foot McTavish under my arm. And every morning I surfed, I would go into the office relaxed and content, with my arms slightly burning and the taste of salt water in my throat, and I thought, *Good way to start the day.*

DAY
MINUS
455

Lisa and I were married in November 2007. I asked Mud to be my best man and Damo, Tim and Richard were groomsmen. I was packing it. We were having an outdoor wedding but it rained all morning, and I wanted to go to the backup venue.

'I'm not moving it,' Lisa said over the phone. 'It will stop raining.' There was a resolution in her voice that I'd come to know. There was a chance our wedding would be held in the downpour. However, towards the middle of the day, the rain slowed to a drizzle. For a brief period, we had clear skies.

I stood in the middle of a forest of pine trees with a hundred others, my shoes muddy, my collar damp. Everyone was ready. The celebrant was smiling at me, and that made me nervous.

Lisa was late. In the photos of those moments, my face looks drained of blood. I look scared, but I wasn't, I just wanted to have a nice wedding, without the rain.

Tim was playing a djembe drum and in the forest it sounded like a heartbeat. I could feel it in my chest, and I could feel my own heartbeat in my ears, playing a faster tempo. There was still no sign of the bridal car. I looked at the sky, and I looked at Mike,

Lisa's brother. He gave me a slap on the back.

'How you doing, Glenn?'

Oh, he was enjoying himself.

My family was close by: my brother Richard, right there, Mum and Dad behind me, Tim drumming, Sarah smiling. And Damo and Mud were standing with me, waiting. Damo told me to slow it all down.

'Take mental snapshots,' he said.

But I was in a fast car looking out the passenger window at a green forest racing by, and the snapshots were blurry.

After a while, a slow-moving car pulled up. Lisa's parents got out, followed by several pink dresses, then some little girls stepped out, and then Lisa. They walked through the forest. The heartbeat in my ears slowed to the pace of the drum beat, and when I caught sight of Lisa walking towards me I knew the image would stay inside me forever: *Beautiful, such a beautiful woman.* She was overwhelmed and overwhelming, and her smile, like mine, was a crazy smile; crazy happy.

We held hands. She was biting her lip to stop herself from laughing or crying, or both, and tears were in her eyes.

The ceremony raced by, rolling through carefully prepared vows. My sister sang. And it ended with a kiss. After the ceremony, we signed the registry with Stu as our witness. A photographer took a photo that would later flash around the world on the internet and in newspapers. And the sun came out.

At the reception I made a speech. I said to Lisa, 'It has been ten months from "hello" to "I do". I remember asking you: "How did we get this close so quickly?" Thanks for looking past the barriers that I've put up along the way. What is it, that you have, that has made me into such a happy person? It's been an incredible thing to have my eyes opened to a new way of looking at the world.'

We honeymooned in Margaret River, Western Australia, and despite all that was good in my world, I arrived there with a lump in my throat that was thick like unchewed meat. I didn't know why it had come, or why it stayed. I tried not to acknowledge it – no anxiety, not on our honeymoon, not when we were supposed to be having a good time. I didn't want it to intrude.

We went to lunch one day, and we had a nice lunch. Then I ordered an affogato and when it came, Lisa stirred it with a spoon.

'What the *hell* are you *doing*?' I spat.

'What's the matter?' she asked, wide-eyed.

That's not me, is it?

Was I that arsehole talking to my wife like that? That was a me under pressure, a me fighting to repress a baffling anxiety. I was just so over anxiety by then. I tried to stay in the present moment, and that helped, but that's some hard shit. I thought back over my life to determine what was causing this constant underlying anxiety; what fearful incident had triggered the whole thing? But I had nothing on that, no insight, and I came to a conclusion: *I'll never find out why, and it doesn't matter why.*

The hard fact was this: anxiety was the penalty I paid for indulging in imagined fears. And oh, fuck me, how I indulged in worst-case scenarios, dwelt on them and spiralled into paranoia. The only solution I had was to ignore fearful thoughts and pretend they did not exist. But that kind of repressing took a 24/7 vigilance, and if I faded even for a second, then anxiety would begin to boil from a simmer and would return more powerfully than I could possibly have imagined. So I realised that these alternatives were unsustainable, they were shit. I'd been thinking myself into a corner, and I had to find a better way.

And so, like my tinnitus, I began to just let my anxiety be. I recognised it was there – I didn't focus on it, or toy with it or indulge it, but I didn't ignore it either. And there was a comfort in choosing to let it ride, and in acknowledging its steaming, stinking outer packaging without actually opening it up. It was hard work, and I failed a few times, but when I got the balance right it worked for me, and though anxiety still built up, it would also pass.

Lisa and I spent a good deal of our honeymoon on the beach and swimming and eating out and sleeping late. I looked at her, my wife, and had to repeat the word to myself, *wife*, to really believe it. I love her so much.

DAY
MINUS
416

In December 2007, my boss told me that I had to go see a psychologist as a part of a new personal development course at my workplace, called Zaffyre. At work I was an energy commodities trader, and traded electricity, and sometimes natural gas, carbon or renewable energies. Mostly I looked at futures screens, and energy contracts, and talked to brokers that I barely knew and pretended to know them well. Trading was a pretend world, but the emotions were real: excitement, despair, revenge, dignity, courage, vacuousness and greed. I had proven susceptible to the dark side of this trading world, because although the money was not mine the responsibility for it was, and I had at times taken the stress of my job home. I had taken it into my evenings, and dinners with my wife, and deep into my sleep with me. And it stayed with me in the mornings as I travelled back to work, with my cheek pressed up against the train window and my forehead vibrating against the pane. And this type of burn-out, I guess, is why my work introduced the Zaffyre program.

Various senior managers in my business unit had already attended Zaffyre, and they had come back with a litany of new expressions: blue thinking, red thinking, green thinking, integral thinking. They talked reverently of emotionally shattering moments of soul bearing and group hugging. There were rumours that some of them had cried. The business unit now wanted me to attend this Zaffyre course.

'What's it supposed to do?' I asked my boss.

'Help you understand yourself. It helps you to listen to what people really mean.'

'I'm not going to talk about my personal issues, though.'

'You will,' said my boss.

'No, I won't.'

'It's a bit of a game.' He looked away dreamily. 'They will get you . . . Jeez, I've seen some people get grilled in there.'

The culmination of the Zaffyre course was apparently a three-day workshop in a hotel conference room where a raft of psychologists would sit you down, with twenty of your work colleagues around you, and fire pointed personal questions at you until you cracked and started crying. Late one night, a previous boss of mine, while on a bender in the city, told me about his experience.

'I didn't tell them anything,' he yelled at me over nightclub music. 'I didn't even answer their questions. I just stared at them. I saved you from it,' he screamed at me. 'I protected you.'

The first personal question I get, the first colleague of mine that looms for a hug, the first talk of love – I am out of there.

I complained to Lisa, 'If they try to make me talk, I will completely explode.'

Before the three-day workshop, I was required to attend several one-on-one sessions with a Zaffyre psychologist at an office building in North Sydney. I sat on a leather couch in a small room, and opposite me was a copy of that leather couch facing back at me, and in between the couches was a coffee table with two glasses of water on it and some pale cashews in a brown bowl. I stared at the nuts.

In came a tall woman with long dark hair. She opened a folder,

inside of which was a psychological profile that was going to cat-
egorise me as either a red (aggressive), blue (achievement) or green
(avoidance) personality, which in turn would decide if I was a selfish
or an integral thinker. She closed the folder.

'So, you're Glenn.'

'Yep.'

'Before we talk about your profile, why don't you tell me what
you think about this course, this journey we are embarking on?'

I cringed a bit when she used the word 'journey', and then I said,
'I don't believe in it. I don't think it, whatever this is, works. Sorry.
I don't mean to be rude. I'm just being honest.'

'I appreciate your honesty.'

'Okay.'

'Go on.'

'I am cynical about this whole exercise.'

'Great!' she replied. 'I love it! Be open about your cynicism, okay?'

'Sure,' I said, rattled.

She pulled out my psychological profile. I saw on the chart a sea
of red.

. . . Not an integral thinker.

'What do you see in these results, Glenn?'

'Red.'

She placed her finger on a different chart.

'What about these?'

'Less red.'

'Notice how much more red you think you are compared to how
your colleagues see you?'

'Hmm,' I said, and cursed myself.

'What do you think that means?' she asked.

'That they don't know me very well?'

She laughed. 'I don't think so. You're very hard on yourself, aren't
you?'

I shifted in my seat. I didn't want to lie to her when I'd just said I'd be honest. Lisa had told me only the week before that I put myself down too often.

'I'm not sure,' I said.

'Okay. We'll come back to that.'

She made a note.

Shit.

'One thing I am interested in,' she continued, 'is this.' She pointed at a green section of my profile that was titled 'Avoidance'.

'What do you avoid?' she asked.

Fear, I thought, and then it came straight out of my mouth.

'Fear.'

She nodded. 'That's a good insight.'

Actually, in only a short time, I came to like this woman, this psychologist. Everything she told me about psychology she backed up with evidence, all scientifically founded, and I saw that she really knew her stuff. Over the next sessions I got comfortable and told her about my anxiety. She got me thinking about the way I spoke to myself – my 'inner critic', she called it.

'You can't let your inner critic run rampant. Stop and listen to what it tells you, don't just let it talk to you unchallenged. Evaluate what it is saying, make an active assessment of it – is it being realistic? If you are unaware of it, it will run your life.'

It was a different perspective. The incessant monologue of my mind was something I had always found uncontrollable.

I eventually attended the three-day Zaffyre workshop. It was intense. I saw a few colleagues cry, and there was hugging. After the workshop, I began noticing how much I would rip into myself. For a long time I had thought it was productive to insult myself, that it would spur me on. Zaffyre got me asking the question: *Is this actually helping me right now?*

DAY
MINUS
394

I bought a 6'6" surfboard; it was thinner and narrower than the McTavish, with a curve in it called a rocker, and it was able to turn in the steepest part of the wave. It had much less foam than my longboard. On flatter waves my longboard would cruise easily over flat sections, but this 6'6" would have to be cut back into the steeper part of the wave. The surf was pumping the first day I ran down the beach with that new board.

I sped into the water. The board sank below the water line. Only a few inches of the nose peeked above the ocean. I'd forgotten that shortboards were like that – my longboard had enough foam to keep me entirely out of the ocean. I paddled, hauling water, feeling like it was treacle. I got out the back with my shoulders burning. It was crowded. Other surfers powered past me on smaller boards than mine, with a paddle power I didn't have. I struggled to catch any decent waves.

Frustrated and buggered, after an hour I went in. I turned back towards the surf and watched a blonde woman catch a left-hander and do four turns before pulling off the wave and zooming back out. I walked home.

'How was the surf?' asked Lisa.

'I struggled.'

'Did you have fun though?'

'Um, sure,' I said.

Not really.

After that attempt, I started surfing regularly. I wanted to get paddle fit. It got religious. I was out there all the time, and I started getting good waves, and my commitment to surfing surprised Lisa.

'How come we never go for walks in the morning any more?'

'Well, how about we go for a walk this afternoon?'

'You're going surfing this afternoon.'

'Oh, yeah. Well —'

'I've created a monster.'

In the sea, I began to recognise faces in the crowd – regular surfers with whom I shared occasional nods of recognition. The morning surf scene was a predictable gathering: young locals, surfers born and bred in the area; old locals, battered veterans on longer boards; the great regulars, who ripped waves apart. The learner regulars, the international visitor regulars, the friendly regulars, the aggressive regulars and the non-regulars made up the rest of the jostling crowd with its arguments and drop-ins. Even so, I still occasionally saw a perfect wave go somehow unridden in a crowd of hundreds.

While at work, surrounded by phones and futures screens and the sounds of typing, I'd check the Aquabumps website, which posts surf reports every day. It'd make me stare at the clock and wonder how early I could leave work to get back in the water, and whether the waves would still be good, and what direction the wind was swinging, and I'd think that, damn, I liked my new board because it had started doing turns that I had forgotten how to do.

DAY
MINUS
318

In March 2008 we went to Shoal Bay, near Stockton Beach, for a long weekend. Lisa and I had been married for four months. I'd turned thirty-three. I felt peaceful and calm; I had a life of surfing and reading, and nothing else feeling urgent or important. Anxious thoughts still registered occasionally, and circled for a while, but then left, and I found I was capable of not engaging with them. Emotional intelligence, my boss called it. Being present, Lisa called it. Whatever it was, I lived each moment better than I had. I really felt all the things I felt, and they did me no harm. I'd arrived in the real world.

I checked the waves at Stockton Beach and they were being jumbled by an onshore wind that beat the ocean into a choppy rage, but the wind soon dropped and it calmed. Lisa came with me and lay a towel on the beach as I walked to the shore. The waves were head-high and wobbly and the water was murky. I knew Stockton was known for great whites, but I gently dismissed this threat, because I hadn't heard of any attacks there. Plus, it was a long beach, and there were already two guys out there.

I strapped my legrope on. Behind me, sand dunes ran off to the west. In front of me, the shore dropped away sharply, then shallowed over an inshore sandbank. There was a channel over near the rocks that I could've used to get out the back, but the paddle through the white water in front of me didn't look difficult. I waded into the sea.

Crossing the inshore sandbank was harder than I expected. The waves breaking over it had some punch and I got stuck there for a while, pushing down duck dive after duck dive. The water was shallow enough that the waves were hammering me, and yet it came up to my chest when I stood up. It was a bugger. I kept paddling.

Good exercise.

A wave pitched into the sea two paddle strokes in front of me. My duck dive was spun upside down by the turbulence and I came up arse first and swallowed foam. Lisa was on the beach watching.

This will be embarrassing if I have to go in and walk around to the frickin channel.

There was a break in the swell. I paddled at full speed, kicked hard for a few seconds, and managed to clear the sandbank before the next wave reared. The rest of the paddle through the flatter section was easy.

Out the back, I sat up and looked around: there was no one there. On the beach I saw two surfers walking up the sand. I was alone. There was a lull and chop washed over my waist. The ocean charged at me and then drained away, the planes of its surface reflecting sunlight brilliantly before an instant later going dark. Swell lifted me up so that I could see the horizon and then dropped me back below it. And it got to me: the murkiness, the quiet, my thoughts, the great white stories.

I'm being watched.

I sat still. I closed my eyes. I reminded myself that the fear was a feeling, just an abstract thing, separate from me. Surfers sometimes refer to sharks as 'men in grey suits': it's a glib way of downplaying them and implying that they innocuously go about their own business and are too busy to take an interest in surfers.

I am not their business.

I told myself this, but my shark fear stayed with me in the water and was tempting me to get out. I paddled to the north – not quickly, just fast enough to keep moving – hearing the chop beating hollowly against the concave surface under my board. I put my left arm on my board, gripping the nose, and kept my eyes seaward as I paddled with my right arm. For some minutes the ocean was flat.

I spotted a rise of swell and rushed at it. I caught it as the lip began to feather. The wave stood up steeper than I expected – it sectioned and broke in front of me, and then flattened out. I came around the wash and cut back, and rode it as it re-formed, and floated over the breaking lip as it closed out near the shore. I dived under the wash and pulled myself back on my board.

That was a decent wave!

I paddled. I felt like I had surfed that wave well, that I was good on it, and I gave myself a massive wrap about it.

This board is great. I can't believe no one is out here.

A wave broke and walled up beautifully as I paddled over its shoulder. Excitement replaced fear, or perhaps just gave it an edge of defiance.

The surf stayed good for thirty minutes. I was joined by a young surfer, and a guy on a mini mal. I didn't think about being watched any more. The wind came up and scarred the sea, and the waves became unruly and harder to ride. I hacked and bounced on a few lesser waves until I was satisfied I'd had the best of it. I caught a re-form to shore.

As I waded in, my board under my arm, legrope gathered in my hand, I turned back to watch the waves crumble under the southerly. A swimmer hopped past me, diving under the wash. I turned again and there was Lisa, waiting on a towel as its edges flapped in the wind.

'How was it?'

'Okay,' I said. 'Although I felt like I was being watched at one stage.'

'Really?'

'Yeah.'

She looked at the sea.

'It's pretty murky.'

'Yeah.'

'It's okay, though.' She smiled.

I knew what she meant.

'Yeah, just something that came up.'

Elsewhere, the great white had turned three years old. It was now 2 metres long from tail to snout, weighing in at around 100–120 kilograms, and was half a metre wide.

I didn't often worry about sharks, and I never worried about them when I surfed at Bondi. Firstly because the chances of attack were slim: there were always lots of people in the water and statistics suggested that someone else was on the menu. Secondly, the shark nets made me feel safe.

Sydney's beaches were netted after a run of attacks in the early twentieth century. From 1900 to 1936 there were seventeen attacks on Sydney beaches, nine of which were fatal. Sydney's nets were introduced in 1937, and since then there hasn't been a single shark-attack fatality on Sydney beaches. As attacks on netted beaches have declined, netting is generally presented as a success by the authorities. However, there is some debate on this point. Other factors may have had an impact on the statistics, such as declining shark populations. Also, shark numbers may have been abnormally high in the 1930s due to meat and lard from the Homebush abattoir flowing into the Malabar sewage outfall – that food source may have contributed to the number of shark attacks.

In 2009, the New South Wales Department of Primary Industry concluded that shark nets are an effective way to protect people. They recommended that netting continue. Their environmental risk assessment found that shark nets posed only a moderate risk to the great white population, a negligible risk to other sharks, and a low risk to marine mammals. But they didn't say what those terms meant — they didn't say what 'low' or 'moderate' was. How low is okay? How low can you go? In 1996, Environment Australia estimated there were fewer than 10000 mature great white sharks left. The New South Wales shark nets have killed 500, or 5 per cent, of that population — is that low or moderate killing? Or is it actually quite a lot?

In hindsight, I really didn't know that much about shark nets. I just knew the nets were there, at Bondi. They kept the sharks out, and they made me feel safe. I didn't know that the nets are only up between September and April each year, and only on weekends and nine other random days each month (if the weather conditions are favourable). I didn't know that nets are not a barrier. They don't cover the whole beach. In fact, they're only 150 metres long, and sit on the sea floor, while the top of the net lies 6 metres below the surface of the ocean. I didn't know that the nets at Bondi had caught only seven great whites, and that some of them had been caught on the beach side of the nets. I didn't know that nets also catch two or three dolphins a year, and two or three sea turtles, and occasional killer whales, and humpback whales, and baleen whales, and seals and dugongs — very few of which survive. Over the period of 1950 to 2002, New South Wales nets killed more than 11500 sharks (including endangered ones).

Ministers of the New South Wales government, after shark attacks, have to answer the question: 'What are you doing about sharks?'

And they say, 'We've got nets.'

And they've been heard to claim, 'Nets break up shark habitat patterns.'

But scientists don't say that. The scientists think they don't know enough about shark habitat patterns to make that claim. The fact is, nets are a fishing device, plain and simple. They catch and kill sharks, and they kill a lot of other species of marine life too. Do they work? Do they stop shark attacks? The scientists can't put their hands on their hearts and tell you that. They just don't know.

Regardless, the nets are here to stay; it's political. In New South Wales, there has only ever been one shark attack fatality on a netted beach. That is a strong statement (weakened by the fact that shark-attack fatality rates have been decreasing, across all beaches, for decades). A politician would never risk taking the nets away. It's a case of shooting first, then doing – nothing. Theoretically, we should be asking questions. But we're not.

We need to manage the nets better. We need more scientific research – tagging studies, information collection, studies looking into migration patterns, and a greater understanding of the environmental variables associated with shark attacks (cold water upwelling, turbidity, salinity, baitfish, etc). That's all missing. If we knew more about that stuff, we might not need nets. The nets are a blunt object: possibly effective, definitely cheap, and deadly.

DAY
MINUS
243

In June 2008, I took Lisa to the Point. Nostalgia drove it; I'd been thinking of it since I'd started surfing again. It reminded me of Luke; it symbolised our youthful friendship. The council had reinstated the sand dunes that had been destroyed by developers. The new dunes were covered in spinifex and pigface, and the beach was narrower than it had been. I was pleased the sand dunes were back, but I wondered if it would stop the Point breaking like it had.

Lisa and I walked out on the rocks. It was cold and we were in jumpers, hands in pockets. The sky was overcast, the surf tiny and only lapping at the rocks. I walked out onto the Point, by myself, getting my shoes wet, while Lisa stood behind me among the tumble of filing cabinet-shaped rocks.

'I'd like to surf here again,' I told her.

And later we had a conversation about regret.

'Remember what happened with Damo?' she said. 'Well, this guy, Luke, you talk about him all the time —'

'Yeah, but I've tried . . . We went out drinking a few times when I was at uni, it was easier to relate when we were plastered. But it was kind of, just, a token thing.'

'Did you talk about your falling out?'

'No. I mean, once we had a stammered conversation, but it didn't make a dent in anything.'

'Maybe you should contact him. It's this one thing. The way you speak about him, it's obvious that you had such a close friendship. If he doesn't want to speak to you, well, at least you were true to yourself.'

Several weeks later, on a slow Thursday morning, I was at work looking at synoptic charts and reading surf forecasts. A large swell was due on the weekend, and conditions were looking good. The swell would be too big for Bondi; it would shut down the whole beach. I wanted to go to the Point. If I got on the road by 5 o'clock Saturday morning, I could be in the water before 7.

I knew Luke taught at our old high school. I looked at its website and, before I'd really thought it through, I wrote him an email.

On Saturday morning, I was in my car by 5 a.m. The Manly wave buoy showed a big increase in south swell. When I drove past Bondi it was still dark, but I could see enough to know it was a solid swell. The sound was big.

When I got to the Central Coast I turned on my phone and checked the address that Luke had given me. I arrived at his place before 6.30, and, although he must have known that I'd kept my hair, because I had seen him around from time to time, he still said, 'Mate, you've still got your hair!'

'Some of it,' I said.

Luke wanted to check the Entrance channel, so we headed out there in his four-wheel drive. It was fully light by then, and I was hoping he didn't want to go in, because it was massive. The swell was raw and breaking all over the place.

Luke leaned over the steering wheel, with some rap thing on the stereo that was not to my taste. I thought about how different we were. I wondered if it was a gulf that couldn't be crossed.

He stared at the Entrance channel. I remembered that intent look. Was it rideable? Was it just rideable? Were there any gems among the closeouts? I'd given up surfing for close to ten years, and this was the biggest swell I'd seen since I started again.

'I've been surfing out here a lot,' he said. 'You see that bank on the north side?'

'Yeah.'

'Pumping. Barrelling.'

There was no one out there. As far as I could see, there wasn't a soul.

'Who do you go surfing with?' I asked.

'Just by myself, mostly.'

'Yeah.'

'Mate, I think it's a bit messy out there,' he announced finally. 'Let's go to the Point.'

I relaxed as Luke swung the four-wheel drive around. The Point wasn't quite as big, though no one was out there either, and no one was out along the whole stretch of beach to the north. There were a few closeouts, but some waves held up. The tide was too high for us to jump off the rock. We would have to paddle out through the heaving white water.

In Luke's garage we changed into our wetsuits.

'Mate, you wearing a short-arm?'

'Yeah,' I said.

'You're gonna freeze!'

We jogged down the quiet street, boards under arms, my legrope tapping against the deck as I ran. The wind was gentle, but stiff with cold. I hobbled over the tarmac, little teeth in the tar snaring my soles. We came down the hill, through the caravan park, over the dunes and onto the beach without seeing anyone. We strapped on our legropes and entered the sea where the beach joined the rocks.

We paddled through a rip along the rocks, duck diving fading white water, and rising and dipping on the unruly surface. Three-quarters of the way out, Luke, in front of me, paused while a set rose skyward out the back and broke. Its white water came to us, dissipating, and we duck dived again, waiting there for a break in the swell. When the sea lulled, we paddled through the breaking zone, racing the next spilling set. Out the back, water surged over the rocks. Foam washed over my board and sand churned to the surface.

'There's a lot of water moving out here,' Luke shouted through the noise. I nodded.

In a lull, we talked about friends we hadn't seen for ages, and family, and all the time we were talking we were shouting and paddling against a sweep that pushed us away from the Point. A set came. I put in hard strokes to get closer to the Point, bumping in the wash off the rocks. A mid-size wave peaked. Luke was in a better position than me, but he sat up and called me onto the wave. I turned. He shouted as I took off, '*Yew!*'

The wave went from steep to vertical in a split second. I skidded down the face and tried to plant a big bottom turn, but the wax felt slippery under my feet and I only managed an awkward turn. But it worked, kind of. I sailed down the line and made another turn and the wave closed out.

I paddled toward the rocks, getting myself back into the rip. I saw Luke get a great wave, turning and hitting the lip easily. He casually kicked out the back of the wave as it closed out the bay.

I attempted to paddle through the breaking zone and was dashing over the shoulder of a wave when a set came through behind. It walled up and detonated. I pushed as deep in a duck dive as I could, but I lost my board and was washed around and upside down, and came up in the foam. Luke was smiling.

When we got out the back, I sat up and said, 'I just got pounded.'

'I saw that,' he laughed.

After our surf, I sat around at Luke's place warming up. We had the best conversation we'd had for many years. I told him a little about my life: the anxiety stuff, meeting Lisa. He had his own stories to tell, his own issues, private things for him. It came out that neither of us, in our youth, had the hardness or coldness that both of us had assumed in the other. I'd never realised how tough some things had been for him, and after that I felt like I understood him better. He was remarkably open, and it surprised me, and I thought, *We're more alike than I realised.*

After that I felt easier around him.

DAY MINUS 103

One day in November 2008, I got off the bus at Bondi and jogged home in my suit. The surf was kind of good – not great, but okay. It was daylight until 8 p.m. I had time to get in the waves. I gave Lisa a quick kiss, and slipped into the bathroom. My board shorts were in there somewhere. I noticed, next to the sink, a peculiar white tube with a little plastic window, and in that window were two blue lines. I picked it up, trying to figure out what it was. I slid the door open.

'Hey, Lis—'

She was standing right outside the door, tears in her eyes.

'Really?'

She nodded.

We had only decided to start trying very recently. It had happened quickly. We were blessed. Lisa held on to me.

'We're the lucky ones,' she said.

DAY
MINUS
2

Lisa and I went to Mexico and the USA over the 2009 New Year break, for a last overseas holiday before the baby came. Was Mexico the smartest place to go with a wife who was twelve weeks pregnant? No. In Mexico City, at high altitude, Lisa fainted. Not great. And she had to be careful with food; gastro when pregnant is a massive no-no. Still, we had fun on the beach at Puerto Escondido, and I got some waves.

We went to New York City and saw Stu, who had moved there for cancer treatment. He was in a bad state. Chemotherapy had all but destroyed his immune system and he was in isolation, unable to leave his small apartment. We spent a quiet New Year's Eve with him, and left sadly. I could see him fighting for his life.

After a few weeks in LA, Lisa had to fly to Europe for work and I was going back to Sydney. Lisa got emotional when we parted at the airport. I figured she was upset because she was heading off pregnant and alone, or maybe just because she was pregnant. Whatever it was, Lisa felt some change coming. We hugged, and I held her. When she left me she was crying and her tears were brutal.

I got back to Sydney in late January and it was warm, 32 degrees. The sea was also warm – 22 degrees. The wind was onshore, and the surf was shit; pancake-flat. It was full-blown summer. There was hope that Sydney would get some refracted north-east swell as Tropical Cyclone Ellie ran at the Queensland coast. Unfortunately, all Ellie created was a huge rain depression in north Queensland that flooded Townsville and Cairns. A mighty high-pressure system sat in the Tasman Sea and blocked any swell-producing weather, and in Sydney the heat, and flatness, just persisted oppressively.

I busied myself packing up our apartment, which Lisa and I had sold, realising we would need more space when the baby arrived. We were moving in with Lisa's parents for a while until we could buy somewhere bigger. I had only lived in the apartment for a year, so my junk factor was low, but Lisa had lived there for seven years and some of the cupboards in that place would only close with brute force. I packed boxes during humid, sticky afternoons, running down to the beach to cool off in the water. That was the way life went for me in the first few days of February 2009: work, packing, sweltering until late.

Lisa arrived home on 4 February, and that afternoon the wind began to howl from the north-east. We had four days left in the apartment, and were too busy for anything but working and packing.

By 8 February, the day Lisa and I were moving out, the wind had been blowing from the north-east for four days. And a funny thing happened – cold water upwelling caused the ocean temperature around Sydney to drop from 22 degrees to 17 – from summery to autumnal. The water became full-length steamer temperature. That night, Lisa and I moved into her parents' house, in Dover Heights, which was on a hill to the north of Bondi. We had been slowly shifting our gear up the hill over the week, and that night we officially moved into the spare bedroom and onto a foldout bed. Lisa, five months pregnant, could barely speak, she was so tired.

Over the next two days, 9 and 10 February, the high-pressure system in the Tasman Sea finally dissipated. A southerly change moved up the east coast. It brought rain, a choppy ocean, and the first dribbles of a building south-east swell.

DAY
MINUS
1

On Wednesday, 11 February, the weeks-long Sydney wave drought broke and messy 2-foot swell arrived at Bondi. Surfers paddled out into conditions that would normally be considered inconsistent and worthless.

I woke later than usual, tired from packing and moving. I heard the wind howling outside and knew that it was an ugly southerly. I surmised, half asleep, that the surf would be junk, and that it would be better in a day or two when the swell got bigger and the wind lighter. I rolled over and went back to sleep with the boxes of our packed-up apartment surrounding the foldout bed.

I saw the surf on the way to work and was pleased to see the white water, but it was woolly and junky and I wasn't missing much.

Work was frantic. A three-hour meeting, twelve people, twenty-four elbows, nine variously coloured coffee cups, each lifted irregularly and religiously and then replaced on the table, a pile of muffins, cake, chocolate biscuits. At noon, I checked Aquabumps. A local surfer was doing a cutback on a reasonable wave.

I felt a pang. I'd possibly missed a decent morning session. I mean, how'd that happen? I'd stopped to watch the surf just to make sure it was shit, and it was. Surfable, but low quality. I'd left Bondi feeling okay about my decision to skip it. But now, having seen Aquabumps, an anticipation started to build in me, a froth, or an itch, or whatever the hell you want to call it. It's a thing that gets my feet tapping and causes a close watching of clocks and a scanning of surf cams. Froth can make me drive wildly, and sprint down the street in my wetsuit; it's a boiling passion that I like and I hate. It doesn't go away. And even at 6 p.m., buried in an unfinished and seemingly untenable spreadsheet, the froth had me thinking that I might be able to get in the water. But, by 7, with various circular references plaguing me, it was too late. It was dark when I got home.

Lisa and I sat around with her parents, lazing on the couch, talking about the kind of place we would like to buy, and the baby. Lisa, her belly swelling, deep in her second trimester, was weary. She lifted my arm, shuffled across the couch and leaned into me.

Lisa's mother, Anne, asked if I'd heard about the navy diver who just that morning had been attacked by a bull shark in Sydney Harbour. He was alive, this navy diver, but on the news they said he'd lose a hand and maybe a leg. It was the first attack in Sydney Harbour for ages. I didn't know many details. I didn't know this was the fourth Australian shark attack that summer, or that it had been a surface attack. I comforted myself that it was probably a deep, deep water attack, and that divers were just more at risk than surfers, you know, being at the bottom and all. I had no idea that most shark attacks are surface attacks. I didn't know that, and didn't want to know it.

'Have you ever seen a shark?' asked Anne.

'No,' I said. 'My friend saw one once, so we paddled in, but I've never seen one. I never want to.' We laughed.

And I never did want to see one either; fuck that. I didn't even want to think about it. I didn't want to encourage the occasional thoughts that crossed my mind whenever I saw a shadow in the water or saw the ocean splashing for no apparent reason. Sharks were out there. I was scared of them. So what? So was everyone. When rare shark thoughts came my way, I'd just close my eyes and tell myself it was okay to have a fear of sharks as long as I didn't let it control what I did.

'They are out there,' I said to Anne, 'but they're not that interested in us.'

This navy guy was a diver, down deep in the harbour – that was a totally different situation to anything I'd ever encountered.

Lisa's parents went to bed. Lisa fell asleep on my shoulder. I relaxed against the cushions, and from where I was sitting I could see across the darkness to the naval ships at the Harbour, only a few kilometres away.

DAY
0

I woke at sunrise. The southerly was still blowing, I could hear it whistling. I woke as if I hadn't slept. Before I got up to go surfing, I rolled over to hug my wife, and when my eyes opened again it was 8 a.m. And I'd missed it. I sat on the edge of the foldout and my lips pursed in a frown.

That was useless.

I wouldn't be surfing today. I had an energy contract to finalise, and after work I was meeting Damo for a beer. I drove past the beach. The waves were bigger, but still washy and choppy.

At work, I got stuck in a frustrating, ongoing contract negotiation. I was edgy, and unsatisfied. Heated discussion ensued, veiled threats, condescending reprisals, pleas, mute on, mute off, long moments. Finally the man I was negotiating with came to an agreement with me, but I didn't internally fist pump, I just sighed.

I checked Aquabumps. Bondi was 5 foot, with a 15-knot southerly making it kind of ugly. Bondi often closes out at that size, but the messy conditions were throwing up occasional rideable peaks. The photos showed a sea of colours: out the back the ocean was dark and white-capped, in the middle the breaking waves were green with brown sand diffused across their faces, and in the foreground was the frothing white water.

Damo emailed me mid-morning. He had to cancel our drink after work. He had a young baby, and that makes all plans subject to change. I understood, and I admit that I got excited: Lisa was going out to dinner with her girlfriends, and documentation of the contract I was working on would be finished by 5 p.m. My evening was free.

I clicked back onto Aquabumps. The wave in the second picture actually looked okay. RealSurf.com was speculating that the swell would not last long. My feet started tapping. I thought about my 6'4" AH, a new surfboard I'd just bought. Its whiteness stopped me every time I saw it perched in the bedroom corner, ready to go.

At 4 p.m., I spoke to Lisa.

'I won't be home that late,' she said. 'Will you be okay?'

The North Head wind station showed the wind drifting to south-southeast at 17 knots. I watched the updates, hoping to see it back off.

It will be surfable . . .

Sunset was at 8.18 p.m. If I finished work at 5, I would have time to get my board and catch a few waves before it got pitch black.

At 5 p.m., there was a problem. The contract documentation was done, but I realised there was another piece of work I needed to complete. I had promised the general manager a slide for his meeting.

Shit, that's going to take an hour.

I jogged out of the elevator at 6 o'clock. There had been a little rain. The overcast sky was threatening the daylight. I weaved through a crowd, skipping sideways past pedestrians. At the train station, I ran down the escalator.

It was almost 6.30 when I got to Bondi Junction. I still had to ride the bus through suburbia and up to Lisa's parents place to pick up my board before driving down to the beach.

The traffic was heavy. The bus was packed and it only meandered along. I stood in the aisle gripping an overhead stabiliser, frustrated by people constantly getting off the bus.

How many times is this bus going to stop?

There were people riding the bus just one stop.

We'll fly once we're on Bondi Road, and if I'm home in twenty minutes, and it takes ten minutes to get my board and drive back to the beach, and then four minutes to put my wetsuit on, that'll mean that before sunset . . .

The bus turned onto Bondi Road, and didn't fly. Instead, it was marooned in a glut of stationary vehicles. After a while, we moved, and then stopped, and then moved, and stopped.

Come on.

As we went past Bondi I saw surfers in the water. I watched the flags on the promenade, gauging the direction and intensity of the wind. It seemed less robust than it had been. Waves arrived. I squinted through traffic, through trees along the median strip, and around the surf club, and I decided that it was worth it. I mean, it was blown out, scattered and lumpy, but worth a paddle.

My feet tapped.

Five minutes from here, eight minutes to get back down to the car park, three minutes to get my wetsuit on.

Come on, come on . . .

I leapt off the bus and landed in front of Lisa's parents' house. No one was inside. Lisa had already gone to dinner. I grabbed my surfboard, glancing at the book on my bedside table. It was a great book, and I'd been gripped by it. A moment of lethargy tempted me.

Read the book.

But then I left, because I already had the board under my arm.

It's probably worth a paddle.

I pulled the front door firmly closed, slid my board into the Jeep and chucked my wetsuit in the back.

I drove through an intersection. It was 7 p.m. The ocean came into view and surfers were crawling over its bumpy surface. I held the steering wheel steady with my forearm and twisted the gold wedding ring off my left hand. I sat it in the Jeep's console.

I parked at the south end of the beach and sat for a minute to watch the sea from behind the windscreen. Light rain flecked silver on the glass. Wind blustered against the car. There were at least thirty surfers in the water. It was 7.05 p.m.

Looks pretty average.

The waves lacked shape. They broke in sections all over the shop. Some waves closed out; others peaked only to fatten, peter out, and turn to mush.

I'll just get four waves, four good ones, and then I'll crash on the couch and read the shit out of that book.

I put my wetsuit on and paddled out. The water was cold. There was rubbish floating about; stormwater had washed plastic into the sea. I paddled towards the line of surfers bobbing up and down. I was 80 metres offshore when I sat up.

I saw Rick Rawlins. He sat the deepest, ahead of a group of other surfers. I didn't know Rawlins personally, but I'd seen him surf;

he was one of the best locals. Through photos on the internet, or through hearing others talk about his surfing, I had put a name to his face. I sat away from the group that he was with. Given that the waves weren't breaking in a consistent spot, I let myself drift south. It was less crowded.

I saw John Grady. He was a regular, about my age. We'd said g'day, occasionally. I did my best to mind his space and to stay off waves that he was in a better position for.

At 7.30 p.m., Shahbaz Roshan, a 35-year-old doctor, arrived home from working in the emergency room of Prince of Wales Hospital. Born in Tehran, he'd come to Australia after a life in England and had surfed almost every day of the six months he'd been in Bondi. Despite the fading light and the murky surf, he jogged out of his apartment with a red 6'4" surfboard under his arm. When he arrived at the south end of Bondi, he noticed dead fish, blue bottles and other debris littered along the shore. He didn't like the look of that, so he walked further north and started to fasten his legrope on the shore.

In Bondi's southern corner, 200 metres from where I was, a French surfer named Mikael Thomas was paddling. Mikael and his close friend Sebastian le Bail were in Australia on a working holiday, learning English, and surfing the New South Wales coast. Mikael was a hero. In 2007, he had saved a man from drowning, a fisherman who had gotten trapped between a rocking boat and a harbour wall. Mikael had dived in to save him and was awarded for his bravery by the president of Ocean Lifesavers in France.

I caught a wave that faded into mushy chop and then I turned off and lay back on my board. I was 40 metres offshore. I started paddling back out. Rick Rawlins had caught the wave before me, and, deciding to go in, he parked himself 20 metres from shore, waiting for a little re-form to come along. He watched me paddling back out.

The great white was four years old. It was likely just passing through Bondi on its way south to Corner Inlet. It was 2.5 metres long and almost 200 kilograms. The shark nets were up. It avoided them. It swam along the inshore channel between Rawlins and the sandbank that I was paddling over. Its diet was changing. It was big enough to start eating seals and mammals.

The water was dark, and, from below, the shark saw movement and a silhouette.

I was 70 metres from shore and 10 metres from a pack of surfers in front of me. I saw a wave coming and changed direction to catch it. My left arm was shoulder-deep in the water. My arm was grabbed.

I didn't feel the teeth. I reflexively pulled my arm towards me. I came off the board and didn't have time to yell before I went under. It was strong. Its aggression was impersonal and savage. Rawlins was the sole witness of the attack: he saw the great white launch at me, and saw its tail, then its dorsal fin, then its head rise out of the water as it shook me, trying to tear off my arm. Ferocious, and in control, the great white shook its head. I couldn't see anything beyond dark water. Before I could comprehend what was happening, I was released. I groped for my board.

The ocean turned red. Blood washed over me. I didn't understand what had just happened, but with my right hand I pulled my left arm onto the deck of the surfboard. For an instant I was bewildered. My left hand was severed, hanging by a thread of skin. The bone stuck out. It had yellow stuff inside it. My forearm was open, gaping, torn along its length. Blood squirted onto the board.

'*Shark!*' I screamed.

The scream scared me, because it was uncontrollable. It leapt out as an unbelieving roar. A ripple of panic swept the crowd. Surfers shot off in every direction. I understood that, but it frightened me. I was alone. I could sense what they were thinking:

You're dead.

I knew the shark would kill me if it came back.

Rawlins saw a wave come towards him. As it rushed to the shore, sucking up water from below and thrusting it forward, it was red.

The shark is coming back.

I scanned the water; it was dark, choppy.

Is this a nightmare?

I knew Lisa would miss me.

I have a few minutes.

Blood was everywhere. I paddled. I thrashed, kicked. My arm on the board was twisted flesh, bloody, open flesh.

It's coming back.

Lisa will have to do it all herself now.

I'll never see the baby.

A sob rose in my throat and I stopped and thought nothing of the shark, and nothing of the blood, and only of my wife and child.

I thrashed. I kicked wildly. I was panicking and I didn't get anywhere. I slapped at the water. My board swung around. I was hit by wash. I stopped kicking.

Too much splashing.

The shark will know. The shark will know that I am . . .

Concentrate. I only have a few strong minutes.

I knew that I could only paddle for a short time before blood loss would leave me floppy and pathetic on my board. An easy target.

Is this it?

I considered stopping and screaming for help.

If I stop, I'm dead.

I was on my own. No one else could save me. The chop, the wind howling, the sea rough and uncooperative; no one could help me. My fear was the fear of nothingness, of a lonely death.

I am not going to get out of this . . .

I looked up at the shore wobbling unevenly before my eyes.

A voice in my mind said, sternly, 'Stop panicking. Don't thrash, paddle.'

It was the voice of my dad.

He was right there.

I slipped my right arm into the water, over and over. I just paddled. Whatever happened, if the shark came back, if my blood ran out, I just had to paddle.

Paddle, head down, watch a spot on the board, paddle, whatever happens, I have my head down and I will paddle.

My breath was out of control. I dug at the water. Breath came shooting out. I got a run on some chop. A wave passed under me. I dipped behind its rise. I was over the sandbank, with sand at the surface. It was a long way. I was tiring.

Paddle.

I sensed the ocean steepening.

Head down. Kick.

I skated down the face of a wave. My partially severed hand rocked on the deck of the surfboard. I rode towards the shore.

I won't die in the water.

I was bleeding badly.

I got away.

My hand looked like it might fall off into the water. It was hanging on, just, so I thought I'd pull it off. Yank it, snap the skin, and hold it in my right hand.

But what if I have to paddle again?

If I ripped my left hand off and held it in my right hand, I wouldn't be able to paddle. So I left it there. I kept it as stable as I could on the board.

The wave had strong, high white water. I looked north. There was a surfer on the same wave, watching me.

'Are you alright?' he yelled.

I don't know.

'Can you call an ambulance?' I called back.

I was close to shore.

To the south, John Grady and the Frenchmen, Mikael and Sebastian, were on the same wave as me. They watched.

The wave dropped me in the shallows, 10 metres from the shore. I stood in waist-deep water. My left arm resting on the board. Dizzy.

'I'm going for an ambulance,' a surfer yelled, racing up the beach.

I held my left arm in my right hand. I lifted it above my head to slow the blood.

James McIntosh, aged twenty-nine, was an off-and-on regular at Bondi and had been surfing since he was a kid. He'd just caught a wave to shore. James began to paddle back out but saw something surprising, something he had not seen before: six surfers catching the same wave and not one of them standing up, all riding it on their stomachs. Someone shouted, '*Shark!*' James was dismissive. He kept paddling. The surfers on the wave coming towards him screamed at him to go in.

It must be serious, he thought.

James turned, and caught a wave in. When he got to shore he saw surfers wading out of the water and dashing up the beach, yelling.

Then he saw me.

Blood gushed down my arm. I held it high, like a torch, and blood ran between the fingers of my right hand as I held my arm together. My left hand dangled against my right hand. I struggled through the water until it was knee-deep. I tried to walk further, but I couldn't.

I got away.

I collapsed in the shallows.

James saw a man stagger. He saw me clutching my severed arm above my head. He watched my board, pulled behind me by the suck of the wave, stand up like a tombstone. I was trapped by my legrope. He saw me drop to my knees.

He walked towards me as I stumbled. Then he was at a trot, and then running, as he realised it was real. James waded into the shore break, released me from my legrope and helped me out of the water. Blood covered his wetsuit. We struggled onto the sand. John Grady arrived then. He made a decision.

'Get him down.'

They lay me on the sand. John held my head and shoulders off the sand. I stared at the sky.

At least I will die on land.

James moved away, yanking at my surfboard, trying to get the legrope off.

The French surfers arrived on the shore. Mikael was only twenty-three, but he was confident and practised at first aid. He detached his legrope from his body board, and then he and Sebastian sprinted up the beach, along the wet sand, leaving their boards behind.

I was wondering how long I could survive before I'd bleed out. I wasn't going to get eaten. I felt good about that. I felt warm. I didn't notice Mikael wind his legrope around the top of my bicep.

This, he knew, was the right place to put a tourniquet, so that it would squash the artery against the bone.

Mikael's face loomed over me. He had an accent. He asked questions. I gripped my left arm in my right hand, a death grip. James had retrieved my legrope and now wound a second tourniquet around my arm near my elbow. I watched my left bicep balloon as it filled with blood.

I said to James, 'Tell Lisa that I love her.'

It hadn't crossed his mind that I might die until I said that.

James replied, 'There's no blood, mate. The bleeding has stopped.'

'She's pregnant,' I said.

A crowd of black wetsuits gathered around me. Shahbaz Roshan arrived. He had dropped his surfboard in the sand and run over. Even though, as a doctor, he'd been exposed to gore before, he thought that my arm looked like something out of a horror movie.

I was in shock. He asked me if I knew where I was. My voice was quiet, but I answered something. John Grady held my upper body off the sand, with my legs stretched out in front of me.

'Lay him down flat,' said Shahbaz.

'Are you sure?' asked John.

'I'm a doctor. Lay him down. Make the tourniquet as tight as possible, and lift up his legs, please.'

Shahbaz wanted my legs lifted so that blood would pool in my upper body and head. That would ensure that my vital organs got enough blood. My heart was beating at 100 bpm, which Shahbaz thought was okay, considering. He knew that if I went into cardiac arrest and needed resuscitating, it wouldn't be good.

The crowd got bigger. A sea of faces, all surfers. I couldn't see through them. Mikael and James were speaking to me, peering at me, asking me questions – what job did I do, had I been surfing long – they kept me talking. I concentrated on my breathing.

The crowd made a decision to carry me up the beach to the promenade, so it would be easier for the ambulance. They lay me on Shahbaz's red surfboard and began to carry me. After a few steps I started to slip off the board and there was a great deal of yelling. They put me back down on the sand. Then they got into position, and before they lifted me again someone yelled, 'Be careful, guys, he's fucken heavy.'

I wanted to say that I was only 90 kilos. I wanted to say, *Keep going. Please.* But I didn't say anything.

On the promenade they put me down and the crowd of surfers was joined by passers-by and joggers. Many of them were trying to call an ambulance. A jogger, on her phone, peered in through the crowd to have a look and then went nuts when she saw my arm. Another jogger knelt down next to me. She was a doctor. She called out for someone to get ice and a friend of mine, Gus, not knowing it was me on the ground, sprinted up to the pub. Another doctor arrived.

He said, 'Can I help? I'm a doctor.'

'So am I,' said someone.

'So am I,' said someone else.

I was quiet. That bothered the doctors. They kept asking me my name and date of birth and where I lived and all this identification stuff that I felt obliged to answer even though it seemed unimportant. I told James, again, to tell Lisa that I loved her.

'Lana?' he said.

'No,' I whispered. 'Lisa.'

'Right.' He nodded, and clicked his fingers. 'Lisa.'

Lisa's number came to me. I told the bystanders. They looked at each other. No one wanted that job.

Lisa was at dinner when her phone rang. She was with three girl-friends at a restaurant in Darlinghurst. Unknown numbers came up on the screen. She didn't answer. The phone rang out.

Gus brought the ice back. I saw him see me. I saw his eyes go wide. I called out to him, but he didn't hear me. He was the only person I recognised. The doctors were looking up the road, the crowd was looking up the road, everyone was looking for the ambulance; fifteen minutes had ticked by. The doctors wanted to get a line into me. They worried I would crash. I called out to Gus. He heard me, and came over to sit by me. We spoke. I don't remember what we talked about. I was happy he was there.

The shark alarm went off.

The police arrived and waved the crowd away. They wore blue gloves. They asked me identification questions. They unwound the tourniquet in an attempt to replace it with a bandage and a support slab, but blood started to piss out everywhere. Shahbaz quickly re-tightened the legrope. A police officer with a short black ponytail sat near me. She said stuff; I don't remember it. She shouted at a cameraman, 'Get out of here!'

There was a big commotion about the cameras. I saw flashes. I didn't care.

It was getting dark. An ambulance arrived. The paramedics took over. The main paramedic wanted to replace the legropes with a long, broad tourniquet. I must have said no, and maybe I got upset, because she started explaining that it was not good to have a tight, narrow tourniquet for a long period of time, and that I needed a long, broad one. I didn't understand.

They unwound the legropes and quickly wrapped my arm in

a bandage. When it was finished the paramedic called out, 'Well done, everyone!'

James stepped back, Shahbaz, Gus, Mikael, Sebastian, John, the jogging doctor, the other doctor, all the surfers there, they all stepped back. The paramedics put me on a trolley and loaded me into the wagon.

'Are you allergic to anything?' one of them asked.

I didn't answer. I didn't know the answer.

'Are you allergic to anything?'

There were cameras pointing at me.

The ambulance left the scene. It left the crowd, and camera crews, and blood on the pavement. Apparently it was a depressing scene. There were surfers covered in blood. They washed under the showers. Journalists began carrying out interviews. People from the crowd, people who didn't know each other, shook hands.

After a while it turned pitch-black. Those people went home. Maybe they had a stiff drink, I don't know. Maybe they called someone to talk about it. I can only imagine.

'You're doing fine,' one of the paramedics told me in the ambulance, but he looked upset. It was frightening. I tried to judge from his face whether I was going to live.

'We've got a bleed!' he yelled.

Two others came rushing over the top of me and began wrapping bandages around me and issuing instructions to each other.

I looked away.

The drive was long and hot. The water in my wetsuit was warm. It was loud and one of the paramedics was calling to the driver to tell the hospital my age, my name.

'Shark bite,' she yelled.

'Mention the "A" word,' she mouthed.

She meant *amputation*. I didn't mind. I knew it was gone.

There was another guy, somewhere, asking questions.

'Are you allergic to anything? Are you in pain? How much out of ten?'

I told him I couldn't feel anything, just a tingle.

'Do you want analgesic?' He mouthed his words slow and loud, like I couldn't hear him, but I could hear him fine.

'Are you in pain?' he asked again.

'No.'

I was numb.

I didn't know where we were going.

Multiple unknown numbers rang Lisa's phone. It annoyed her. Then she thought, *Something is wrong*. She walked outside to listen to the messages. Just then, another unknown caller rang. She answered. It was a nursing sister from St Vincent's Hospital. The sister told Lisa that her husband had been attacked by a shark, and that he was alive.

Lisa collapsed in the gutter.

She can't remember the exact words. She heard that I was alive, for now. Her best friend, Georgia, also four months pregnant, helped her walk to St Vincent's, which was only a few hundred metres away. Georgia had to support Lisa as they walked towards the hospital, past the traffic on Victoria Street, in the dark, past ambulance lights, crying, shaking.

The trolley jerked out of the ambulance. The lights, the hospital lights, were so bright and white, and I was on my back, and various heads appeared above me and then left again.

The paramedic spoke to a doctor in a coat, saying that I had been attacked by a shark. This seemed like old news. I was rushed along a white corridor, under fluorescent lights. I watched them shoot by over the top of me.

I'm floating.

The paramedic and the doctor ran alongside me.

'Left arm,' said the paramedic. 'Not allergic to anything,' she added.

Doors and people flashed past. I was warm. In my wetsuit.

It's keeping me together.

'Shark bite,' shouted the paramedic.

The doctor was writing, scribbling, engrossed.

I could feel a tingling, like I had slept on my arm.

'Only tingling,' she yelled.

I thought it would hurt more.

I thought it would feel like being stabbed.

There was a tightness in my hand.

Why didn't the shark come back?

I held still, not wanting to spoil anything, desperate to go where they were taking me. The trolley swung into a white room with white walls, crowded with people in white gowns. I was the only one in black. They looked ready.

I was parked in the middle of the room. Above me were two massive lights from outer space, which shone down on me. Those orbs shone, and the doctors and nurses swarmed on me.

'Am I going to die?'

My throat was thick and no one heard me.

'Hello,' said a doctor with stubble and wearing a white gown. 'Are you in pain?'

He asked me questions I can't remember. I'm sure he would have asked me if I was allergic to anything. That was their number one question. He explained what the people in the gowns were doing. There must have been ten of them. I don't recall a word of what he said. I saw a young woman with short dark hair put a needle in my right foot. I knew she was putting a 'line' in; a line for blood. She was stoked when she got it in. Apparently it's hard to get a line into the foot.

The doctor apologised to me. 'We are going to have to cut off your wetsuit, mate,' he said, and they all began to scissor in unison.

Don't worry.

I'd had that tattered short-arm steamer for ages. I wanted a new wetsuit, but was waiting to clear it with Lisa (and expecting resistance). I knew that I would be nude on the table, under the lights, with all those people around me. It didn't bother me, it was just a thought that came by and then left.

'I'm going to give you morphine,' said the doctor.

A weight came onto my chest.

'Something's wrong,' I told him.

'That's the morphine,' said the doctor. 'It feels like pressure on your chest. That's fine, it's normal.'

'Am I going to live?'

He paused for a second.

'Yes.'

The word was tangible to me. Like I actually felt it rather than heard it; it left a pulp on my tongue that I scraped off with my teeth. How palpable was the relief! I relaxed. I felt welling happiness, but it was stopped by a zoom of pain that rushed into my arm and had me writhing on the table. With the fear gone, pain came to replace it. It turned my relief right into hell. The ache was unbearable. I was unable to stop my legs from jerking. They told me to settle down, and I held my breath, but the pain was searing. It was the deepest ache I had ever experienced. Fuck, it felt like I'd had my arm cut off.

'Breathe, mate,' said the doctor.

An anaesthetist was introduced. I remember that. She was a woman, a young woman, and she was confident. I have no idea what she said to me. She asked questions, but I have no idea if I answered them. I didn't want to cry out or be impolite.

The anaesthetist began to put me under. And, sweet Lord, how I wanted to be under. The pain was excruciating. The doctors looked down at me. I thought the hand would go. It was mostly off already. The anaesthetist put a mask on my face. I stared at the bug-eye lights above me and breathed. The room was quiet apart from the rasp of the respirator.

I would go out, and I wouldn't feel it. I would wake without remembering. I would wake out of pain. I would wake with the hand off, and my wife beside me.

'Deep breaths,' they said.

White robes moved silently about the theatre. Steel bug eyes looked at me as I slipped into oblivion.

Dr Kevin Ho arrived home after having just finished an operation on Paul de Gelder, the navy diver who had been attacked by a bull shark in Sydney Harbour. Kevin got a call that another shark-bite victim had arrived at St Vincent's. He was back at the hospital in twenty minutes.

When he saw my hand, attached by a 3-centimetre band of dermal skin, he was surprised. The wound looked clean. I was stable, so Kevin took his time. He took photos. He thought hard about his options – which were, of course, also my options. When sharks bite, they rip and twist to get through the appendage of whatever soul they have in their teeth. This ripping and twisting causes the vascular structures in said appendage to break unevenly. Then the blood vessels collapse into red mush. A quick amputation with a circular saw is better than a shark bite, as it leaves the ends of the vessels cleanly cut. So when Kevin saw my arm he was surprised: it was a surprisingly clean amputation.

I can put that hand back on, he thought.

The pre-surgery photos of my arm are not great. The arm is pale and lifeless. It doesn't even look like an arm. The flesh and bone is confusing; which bit goes with which other bit is difficult to determine. It looks like chewed veal ravioli.

Kevin decided to have a crack at reattaching my hand to the mush.

When Lisa arrived at St Vincent's, I was in theatre. They told her I would live, but they said I'd lost a lot of blood.

She told Lisa that I would lose my left arm.

'From here,' the sister said, pointing to her shoulder.

Lisa felt hot. A minute later she was freezing. She rang my dad. It was a struggle for her to say the words. Too shocked to cry, she was shaking, boiling hot and frantic.

She told him: 'Shark attack.'

She could say no more.

The nursing sister took the phone.

'Your son has injuries to his left arm and shoulder. It doesn't look good.'

Mum heard this and was lost in hysteria. Dad calmed her, then threw some clothes into a bag. They arrived in just over an hour. Lisa and her parents were in the waiting room. My brother Richard arrived also. They talked about things none of them can remember. Lisa watched nurses wheeling patients along linoleum corridors. Every time the hydraulic doors hissed, her eyes flicked to the doorway, hoping for news. She tried to stop thinking about me dying.

St Vincent's trauma director, Dr Tony Grabs, came to see my family. Tony had done the initial part of my surgery, stabilising me, and then handed over to Kevin Ho. Tony explained that my left arm was intact above the elbow, and that I had suffered a full amputation of my left hand, but that I was okay.

My family were relieved.

The hydraulic doors hissed. Kevin Ho came into the waiting room and introduced himself as a plastic surgeon. Lisa thought that he looked too young to be in charge and she wondered why I needed plastic surgery. Mum, a nurse, and Dad, a doctor, knew what Kevin meant. The term 'plastic surgeon' covers doctors who work on cosmetic procedures (boob jobs, facelifts), but also the gun doctors who undertake reconstructive procedures like microsurgery.

Kevin said he had come in expecting to just amputate my hand; to just scissor the remaining 3 centimetres of skin, saw off some bone, pull the skin over the end, and sew. However, he'd decided to have a go at reattachment. He said that it may have been the best work he had ever done, and miraculously blood had started to flow back into my hand. He still had a lot of work to do. He was not sure how it would go, but he was now going to reconnect the vasculature (veins and arteries), and would leave the muscles and tendons until later. He had removed the bones from my wrist to make space to get the ends of the vasculature together. So, if my hand did reattach, the wrist would be fused. My status had gone from 'He's alive, now' at 8 p.m., to 'He'll lose his whole arm' at 8.15, to 'We are reattaching his hand' at 1.30 a.m.

A night nurse brought some blankets and led my family to a small, brightly lit, windowless waiting room with an old vinyl lounge and a few plastic chairs. Lisa lay on the couch. Our mothers rested on the chairs. Our dads lay on the floor. None of them slept very well. The surgery took fourteen hours.

DAY
PLUS
1

My eyes opened. Lisa's face was soft and beautiful, but with sad eyes. She smiled so kindly and held my hand. I tried to speak.

'Don't,' she said. 'There's a tube in your mouth.'

I traced words onto her hand, but she didn't understand, and she cried. I wiped her tears away. I was with her, and that's what it had been all about in the moments when my life was in question. Now that hell was gone. I breathed slowly and the rhythms of our breathing matched.

I was supine, with my left arm on a stack of pillows and bandaged. My throat was filled with a tube. The lights were bright, the room quiet. There was a nurse with brown hair wearing blue pyjamas.

I pointed at my arm.

'They reattached your hand,' she said.

Lisa remembers that I broke down. I don't remember.

'You're okay, boy,' said Dad, and he smiled like he was proud.

As my eyes closed and I fell through the room, I heard my mother whisper, 'I knew you would make it.'

I floated on the border of consciousness, hearing slippered feet on linoleum. Then I woke with something enormous down my throat. There was a tube inserted into my trachea for anaesthesia. They shouted it: 'You're intubated!'

I could feel their hands on me.

'Glenn! You're intubated!'

Fuck intubation, whatever that was. I wanted the tube out. I could feel it deep in my body. My gag reflex was squeezing it. But they wanted the tube in, because Kevin Ho was considering taking me back into surgery. If my hand died, he was going to take me straight back into theatre and lop it off.

'Richard and Sarah are here,' said Lisa.

I shook my head.

'No?'

I pointed.

'Okay, you want the tube out first.' Lisa turned to the nurse. 'Please, take it out.'

The nurse had to check with an intensive care unit doctor. Apparently this was a different doctor to Kevin Ho. In fact, in the ICU there was a Fraternity of doctors, and one of this Fraternity came in and pinched each finger of my reattached hand. I couldn't feel it. Then he called Kevin Ho and they had a chat, and Kevin agreed it was okay to remove the tube. So the ICU doctor extubated me at midday; hand over hand, he pulled the plastic tubing out of me, and I felt it flap against my oesophagus, ride roughshod over my gag reflex, and come wetly out of my mouth.

I told Lisa I was okay.

'I can't believe it,' she said and her tears fell. 'I thought you were going to die.'

'I was lucky.'

'How did you get in?'

'I got a wave,' I said. 'You were all I thought about.'

I told her about the attack. My parents listened too. They had only heard the news reports and the police had been saying that I was rescued in the water. I told them that I never saw the shark. I told them what I knew.

'I caught the best wave of my life,' I added, and they were quiet.

Lisa never stopped crying through that story, but she needed to know.

'You did good,' Dad told me.

Richard and Sarah came in. Richard's smile was frozen. Sarah looked upset, but resolute. Later Damo was there, and Mud. I was drifting and the room went out of focus.

My hand, they saved my hand.

I held Damo's hand.

'I don't know if we've ever held hands before, mate,' he joked.

It was the last thing I heard before it all went blank.

I was visited by two plastic surgeons, a surgical resident, various ICU doctors, a team of pain specialists, and a physiotherapist. That's the foundation of the intensive care Fraternity. The Fraternity inserted a ketamine bomb into my belly. Ketamine bomb insertions were rare, so everyone gathered around to watch. St Vincent's is a teaching hospital, and all the trainee doctors are keen to see new shit. A young, confident bloke put a blue balloon inside a glass chamber of clear liquid. He then stuck a needle from the chamber into my stomach.

'There you go.'

He rested the bomb against my waist.

'Thanks.'

Ketamine (street name 'Special K') dissociates the conscious mind from the senses.

'If you have hallucinations, just go with them,' said my nurse. 'Don't resist.'

The Fraternity laughed. My parents laughed. Lisa laughed, and I laughed too. I was so happy to be alive, every joke was funny, every moment sweet and vivid. Fuck, it was good to get away from that shark. I was high.

The ketamine was layer one of my analgesic. I also had an intravenous line delivering shots of morphine every time I pressed a blue button. The Fraternity told me to press the morphine button whenever; I could self-administer up to 10 milligrams in an hour. I was also being given oxycodone, gabapentin (for nerve pain), various sedatives (diazepam, valium) and, yeah, a couple of Panadol. The Fraternity thought that a sudden hand detachment and subsequent reattachment would be pretty painful, but I wasn't feeling nothing.

They gave me twenty-three bags of blood – 6.5 litres in all. My entire blood volume went in and out of me, because my left arm had been left open to bleed. Lisa stayed with me, while outside it got dark. I tried to speak but I couldn't, so I watched her until I fell away.

Everyone was concerned about Lisa, but I'd only vaguely noticed it. Lisa had held it together in front of me, but inside her was turmoil and panic. And everyone was worried about how it might affect the baby. The Fraternity organised an emergency scan and the scan gave the baby the all clear, but a fear that the baby was hurt would stay with Lisa for the rest of her pregnancy. That night, though, when Lisa was falling asleep, as if to say that everything was okay, the baby started kicking for the first time.

DAY
PLUS
2

I slept fitfully. It was the noise: beeping drips, trilling defibrillators. And the nurse woke me every few hours to take observations, of my blood pressure, temperature, etc. And I had dreams, and every time the shark came at me I jerked awake.

Morning came, and over the other patients I saw a wall of windows and through them the city, ablaze, reflecting sunlight.

My hand is off.

The room pitched. I blinked the dizziness away. A nurse asked if I was having hallucinations, and I said no. I didn't mention the shark dreams; I figured they were obligatory. She told me to take Coloxyl.

'Pardon?'

'It's for bowel support.'

'Bowel?'

'Morphine causes constipation. You need to go to the toilet.'

'I'm fine,' I said. 'I don't need to go.'

She slipped a bedpan under me.

'No, not while I'm on my back,' I protested. 'That's unsanitary. Horizontal is not the way nature intended.'

That was when she told me about the catheter.

'Pardon?'

From under my bed she lifted up a half-full plastic bag of urine, and showed me the tube leading between my legs.

'It doesn't hurt,' she assured me.

I sank low. Disgust coiled. Was I that weak? The catheter proved I was disabled. Before the catheter, I'd been mobile. If there was a fire, I could have, through a morphine haze, scampered down the flaming ICU corridors. But there was no way I could run with a dangly catheter between my legs. If I tripped on it – what would it pull out?

'I don't want a catheter,' I said.

But the nurse had turned away. Then her blue pyjamas turned green and pink, and pimples of white light bloomed on her back, and the morphine hissed.

When I woke again, people were staring at me. There was a woman with auburn hair, and a man in white. The woman came close and said, 'What is it?'

Everything swam.

'Are you okay?' asked Lisa.

I could only blink at her. A lump grew at the base of my throat. I opened my eyes wide.

She said, shrilly, 'What is it?'

'Hallucinations,' the Fraternity told her.

'Relax,' they said.

Dad came in. He calmed Lisa and me down; just him being there was enough for that. He cast a practised eye over my set-up and explained each of the tubes to us. I had a cannula in my jugular to give me blood and heparin, a blood thinner, and on top of that was taped a chunk of square plastic with several other tubes dangling out of it. There was a cannula in my right wrist to meas-ure blood pressure, and one in my right forearm for something else. I had a cuff on my right bicep that tightened regularly; I don't know why. Leads were taped to shaved patches on my chest to meas-ure my pulse and cardiac rhythm. Inflatable bandages around my calves regularly filled with warm air to stop deep vein thrombosis. My left arm, propped up on pillows, was heavily bandaged, with only the purple tips of the fingers showing, and had plastic-backed mats, called Blueys, underneath it to soak up the blood oozing out of my still-open forearm. The Blueys got taken away when they began dripping blood on the floor. Over my left arm was a mat filled with warm air called a Bair Hugger. I had the ketamine bomb in my abdomen, and down below was the catheter. I had an oxygen line in my nostrils. There were two remote controls on my chest, one with the morphine button and one for the TV. And every movement I made caused tension in various plastic tubes, and led to uncom-fortable entanglements. The tubes were all over me. The cannulas irritated, and, oh fuck, the Bair Hugger made me hot, and it was all too much, and I pressed the blue morphine button and drifted somewhere behind my eyelids.

The attack was on the front pages of all the newspaper: 'First shark attack at Bondi in eighty years'.

The Minister for Primary Industries told the populace not to go in the ocean at dawn or dusk. Then he dusted his hands like he'd done his job, and no one did what he said, and everyone still swam at dawn and dusk. The newspapers interviewed seasoned fishermen who had been (allegedly) expecting a shark attack, and there was a tone in their comments that I took personally, as if they were say-ing, *You brought this on yourself, you idiot.*

That got to me.

Lisa tried to calm me down, but I was well in it.

'Prick fishermen don't have to be all righteous about —'

'It's okay,' she said, and grew anxious.

And so I swallowed the anger down hard.

The media was beaming our wedding photos around the world, and it was distressing for Lisa, a private woman, to have the details of our personal lives scattered so randomly to the strange masses.

A public relations representative from the hospital came to visit my family in the ICU waiting room. He was getting more calls than he'd ever had; *60 Minutes* had rung him personally. Personally! Shark victims – whoa!

As chance would have it, he knew Lisa through a mutual acquaintance.

'Hi!' he beamed. 'How's your friend Kathy doing?'

Lisa hadn't eaten; she couldn't eat because she felt sick. She leaned against the wall, passing her hand over her round belly. She stared at the PR man, then turned away without answering. My dad told him that they were not planning to speak to the media.

I was in theatre, where Kevin was peeling the dermal layer of skin off my hand. After removing the dead tissue, Kevin sat with me in the ICU.

'If your hand lives for ten days, the capillaries will regrow and you'll keep it,' he explained. 'It is going to be tough, though. Today is day one.'

Kevin was giving me a blood thinner to help the circulation in my hand. As the hand had emptied of blood, the capillaries had collapsed and died. Without them, the blood pumping into my hand got trapped in there, and so was making the hand swell like a balloon; 'congestion', Kevin called it. It had to be bled out, and that was why he had removed the skin. He had also left my forearm open, unzipped, so that it would bleed. The Blueys were saturated with blood.

'Even if we only save your thumb and index finger,' Kevin continued, 'it will be more useful than a prosthetic hand.'

To manage the bleeding, he was regularly measuring my haemoglobin level, trying to keep it above 80 g/L (normal level is 130 g/L). When it got below 80, they gave me a bag of blood. The bleeding was a balancing act. If the rate I was given blood thinner was too high, I would bleed uncontrollably. But if it was too low, the blood would clot in my hand.

Put up a good fight. I've got to put up a good fight.

As my family were preparing to leave for the night, a journalist approached them in the ICU waiting room.

'Are you Lisa?'

'Yes.'

'How are you feeling? Would you like your photo taken?'

She had been crying for hours and was too exhausted for the confrontation, and she didn't want her picture taken. But they got a photo of her anyway.

Kevin finished checking my fingers, and then rewrapped my bandage. I liked Kevin Ho. He was young, hardworking and enthusiastic. He had a young child, I was about to have one: we had things in common. He was in uncharted territory, trying to reattach a shark-amputated hand. But he was having a crack, and I appreciated his tenacity.

'Your wife said you don't smoke.'

'No,' I said.

'Ever?'

'No.'

'Good,' he said. 'I don't think we could even try this otherwise.'

Many of the Fraternity in the ICU had been asking me, politely, if they could look at my hand. And they had pored over it like it was a rare species of animal, and that was fine. I was okay with being the human attached to a potential surgical marvel. But Kevin believed that my mental state was the most important thing in saving my hand, and his manner was subtle and sensitive. Kevin was passionate about saving it and it would be a medical miracle if he succeeded. My hopes were invested in him. I watched his face while he examined me, hoping for a smile, and grimacing when he grimaced.

Ten days; one gone.

When Lisa got home, there were photographers waiting on the lawn.

'My God,' she said.

Her father nearly ran over one of them as he parked. Lisa hurried inside with a towel over her head.

DAY
PLUS
3

Overnight my temperature spiked and sleep came only in twenty-minute bursts – shots of sleep. At 7 a.m., the nursing shift changed. I told my new nurse that the Bair Hugger on my arm was torturously hot. She took it off me for a few minutes and gave me an ice cube. She was great like that.

'These are for you,' said the Fraternity, holding out some flowers.

The card was from Paul de Gelder's mother, Paul being the navy diver who was fighting to save his right leg after having had his right hand amputated. I was touched. The nurse pointed to a bloke four beds away.

'That's Paul.'

He was sitting up. He had a shaved head and he looked happy. He waved a piece of floppy toast at me.

'G'day, mate,' I shouted.

'G'day, buddy.'

We yelled across the ICU, but our conversation was drowned out by alarms and phones and the rolling wheels of carts and the morphine holding down our brains. My throat was a dust bowl and my voice was gravelly.

'How are you?'

'I can't hear you,' he shouted.

I couldn't speak any more.

'Did you get the flowers?' he yelled.

I gave him a thumbs up. He smiled. That was the last time we spoke while we were in the ICU together. The nerves in his leg were extensively damaged, beyond repair, and he decided to have the leg amputated. After that, they took him away.

The ICU was active. Blue pyjamas and white lab coats. Visitors wept. Gowned, arse crack-showing patients shuffled around holding drips. A TV sat 3 feet above my head, supported by a metal beam, but the words coming from it were gibberish. This TV stretched its metal neck towards me until it hovered 2 inches from my face and I could feel my breath bouncing off its screen. My eyes drifted away, one of them wide open, the other closing intermittently.

Lisa came in. She'd had no sleep, but was determined to smile. She'd been reading the newspaper; there was a picture of her on page two.

'It's the worst photo,' she said. 'And the photo they have of you, on the front page . . .' She shook her head. 'It's a shocker.'

And that was our first good laugh in hospital, just with each other. I gave her some cheek about her photo until I drifted off to sleep with her holding my hand.

I woke up when a young, thin man, in green pyjamas, leaned over me.

'Hi Glenn, I'm Quan. I'm a plastics registrar, working with Dr Ho.'

Quan was a doctor who was not quite a plastic surgeon, because becoming a plastic surgeon takes a lot of study. The Fraternity had told me that the 'Plastics' were the top guns.

'The Plastics are living the dream,' they said.

Quan was nimble. His agile hands dug into my bandages, pinched my fingers and scraped them with a razor. Quan said that life in the ICU was a rollercoaster.

'Be ready for some bad days,' he warned.

Then he said that my hand looked congested. Kevin Ho came in. His mouth set in a line and I judged from his face that my hand was not doing well. I took in a long breath. Lisa told me it was okay. Things changed so quickly – something good happened (hand good!), then something bad (hand shit!). There was never time for any relaxing breathing. No breath stayed in: it either came out in short bursts, huffs of relief, or in unhappy closed-eyed sighs.

I'll be okay. No matter what. I'm alive.

Then straightaway I disputed that thought and started yelling at myself:

Why me?

Pause.

Why me?

I tried to stop asking it. I knew it would drive me insane.

Kevin decided to take me back into surgery. He told me that he might have to amputate.

My gut tightened. Lisa was there and my parents came in, and I tried to toughen up, but I was shivering.

'If I lose my hand, it's okay. I'm lucky to be alive,' I said.

That was just made-up bullshit, though – those words had no substance at all.

Quan put a form on my lap: 'Consent for Medical Procedure'. I didn't bother reading it. I just signed. It gave them permission to cut off my hand if necessary, I knew that much. On the monitor my heartbeat was 120 bpm. Lisa stood behind the curtain so that I wouldn't see her crying. I called her in, and she sat by me and put her head on my chest.

'It's okay,' I said.

The Fraternity wheeled me into the operating theatre. It was cold. The theatre was kept cold to stop bacteria growing. They put a warm blanket on my chest. Everyone was in green gowns, and they had all been at my first operation and they said I wouldn't remember them. I didn't.

'You're a surfer?' asked one of the doctors.

He pulled down his mask and smiled, and it was a sad smile on his face. He probably knew that my hand would have to be removed.

They put a mask over my face. I recalled the first time I ever went under general anaesthetic, during a knee operation when I was twenty; I'd been worried then and the doctor had put his hand on my shoulder as I was going under. 'You'll be right, mate,' he'd said.

My family sat in the ICU waiting room. The hell of being conscious is the waiting. Lisa was anxious, my parents were quiet; Richard and Sarah were there, and Lisa's parents, her brother and sister too. All quiet, nothing to say, really. They waited eight hours.

At 6 p.m., Kevin Ho walked in and told Lisa that my hand had not looked good when he opened it up. He'd found that a major vein was blocked, but when he'd cleared the obstruction my fingers went 'magically' pink, indicating a healthy blood flow.

I woke at 7 p.m. Kevin had saved my hand. Lisa smiled, my parents hugged, Richard and Sarah hugged, and everyone joined in the hug. I went to run a hand through my hair, but the tubes stopped me.

'Far out,' I said. 'I can't believe it.'

For the second time I'd woken and found my hand still attached when I was sure it would be amputated. I exhaled in relief, though something in my breath was hollow. I had just borrowed heavily from a dwindling stock of luck. I said to Lisa, 'I don't want to get too happy.'

She understood.

Mum and Dad were jubilant, though. Their happiness washed over them freely, but mine was tempered by doubt. I had lost some faith in my hand. It was fragile. I had never considered what life might be like one-handed, but I began to think about it then.

Put up a good fight, I thought.

But there was another voice, a voice of caution, a voice I hated, and it said, *Don't get happy.*

Lisa sat near me, her face close to mine, and in her eyes I thought I could see some part of what I was feeling, some of the same fear. But she never mentioned it. She only said, 'It's so amazing.'

She put her face against mine.

'It's so amazing.'

Kevin had repaired the remaining muscle in my arm and grafted the two remaining nerves back together. But they would take months to heal, if they ever did, and the third major nerve was just not there any more. He had removed a further layer of skin from the hand as well. I was down to the basal layer, whatever the fuck that was. When the nurse undid my dressing, it didn't look like skin, it looked like the inside of a mouth. It was sickening, and Lisa had to stand outside the curtain while it was being treated.

Lisa and I watched the comings and goings of the ICU as it got late. I put my hand on her belly.

'Did you feel that?' she asked.

'Nah.'

The baby's kick was very soft.

'I'm so sorry,' she said.

'Why?'

'I should never have gone out to dinner that night. It was my fault.'

She wept.

'It was no one's fault,' I said. 'It was just a thing that happened. Please don't blame yourself.'

I held her until she left, and was sad to see her go.

That day they'd given me 9 units of red blood cells, 4 units of plasma and 1 unit of platelets, plus during the operation 3 litres of Hartmann's solution and half a litre of Gelofusine. So 8.5 litres of blood volume replacement – more than a body's worth.

DAY
PLUS
4

In the early morning, a slender nurse with a trimmed beard came on shift. He was professional and distant. My bed was wet with blood and I'd had zero sleep; it was the beeping, whining, screaming alarms, the cardiac arrests, and the bloke in the next bed calling for a bedpan every fifteen minutes. It was a circus tent. I was more tired than I'd ever been.

'Get us a pan!' yelled the pan man in the next bed.

I saw his face grimace. It was his third time in the ICU. He was a regular in a place in which it was not a great place to be a regular. He was destitute. The Fraternity told him he would die if he had to come in again.

'Have you been smoking?' they asked him.

'Nah.'

'But you did smoke yesterday?'

'Oh, yeah, well, then.'

'So you have been smoking?'

'Only when I'm given a smoke.'

'You can't smoke at all. Your lungs are extremely frail.'

'Yeah, but what can I do when they fuckin offer'n me!'

He coughed and the Fraternity leaned him over as he spat green crap into a clear plastic bottle, and I watched it slide down the side of that jar. Poor bastard. Sometimes we said g'day, that guy and me. I felt for him. He had a wife that never visited. She may have been a delusion.

Lisa came in early. She sprinkled sugar on my cereal. She was upset.

'Can we talk?'

I shuddered. *That tone.*

I stifled an *Oh what, for Christ's sake . . .*

She said that we didn't have any alone time.

Not now, Lisa, please.

She missed being alone with me. The Fraternity would only let two people in to see me at once, so Lisa spent long periods by herself in the waiting room while others were visiting. And when she was with me, it was with other people. She missed me. I didn't understand. My compassion had gone. I blew up, and it was unstoppable.

'I can't deal with this, Lisa,' I said harshly.

We stopped talking abruptly and then my nurse came to say that he wanted me to have some quiet time, and Lisa left. Then the morphine miasma cleared momentarily, and I remembered that she was pregnant, that I was supposed to be looking after her, but all that had changed because now she was looking after me. I regretted the way I'd spoken to her.

My fingertips were poking through bandages, purple, oozing, bloated. I turned away and watched the news. Apparently there were no surfers at Bondi. It was part shark anxiety, but mostly the waves were shit. Still, I knew the surfers would go back soon. Shark attacks make a horrifying impression, then they fade, and surfers go surfing; that's the nature of it. In 2008, a sixteen-year-old surfer was killed by a shark at Ballina and I had been upset by that attack – he was just so young. His death left a lasting impression on me, but I didn't let it stop me surfing. It had seemed so far away from my life.

At lunchtime I asked everyone to leave so that I could be alone with Lisa. And then she and I sat together, just us, and were happier.

'Do you still want to live by the beach?' she asked me.

'No,' I said.

'Me neither.'

And then we sat quietly, listening to the ICU.

There was a young guy with Crohn's disease just down from me. His name was Matt and he was twenty-five. He was wasting away: really sick, really pale, and thin. He had a girlfriend called Grace, who was young too, and she came in and Lisa said hello and smiled at her – they had already become friends. Grace was in the ICU from morning to night, rubbing Matt's feet, holding him, helping him eat. It was hard to see the two of them like that, right on the brink of life. I have visions of them still.

Quan introduced me to Michael, a tall bloke in his late twenties who was also training to become a Plastic. They were both Kevin Ho's students. They said my hand looked congested again and they suggested I press the morphine button, because Kevin had sent them to try to cannulate a vein in the back of my hand. It sounded important. The morphine syringe hissed. They offered me further sedation. I dribbled.

As they dug around in my bandages, their quiet discussion became intense. I could sense their frustration. I gave a few grunts of encouragement.

Quan lamented, 'The veins have collapsed.'

I was upset. I believed that a cannulation, to draw off the purple hypoxic blood, might save my hand.

'Hmm,' they said.

'Looks like a vein?'

'We can't get a cannula in that,' replied Quan.

I cleared my throat.

'I reckon I can,' said Michael.

I grunted.

'Nah,' said Quan.

Come on.

'I'll give it a go,' Michael said.

I grunted ecstatically.

Michael had his tongue poking out the side of his mouth.

'Quan,' he said, 'I am legend.'

Michael had cannulated the un-cannulatable. I sighed a gust of morphine breath. They grinned brilliantly.

Michael attached a bag to the cannula and it filled quickly with 50 millilitres of purple blood. My nurse was instructed to draw off 40 millilitres of blood every hour. Quan leaned over me with a gentle smile and said they were going to use leeches to suck the rest of the blood out of my fingers.

'Good one,' I said, laughing.

Hand on for two days. Eight days to go.

I drifted into exhausted slumber and sensed a giant roach crawling on me. I scratched after it, chasing it over my body. When I woke, at 2 p.m., there was blood on my hands. The nurse was looking at me. I had pulled out my jugular line. It had been stitched in but I'd ripped it out, and the needle was now jutting out of my neck like a pencil that a magician is about to push into his eye. And there was a bit of panic, because my blood was thinned to the consistency of cordial and there was this hole in my artery. A young ICU doctor came rushing in. She decided to insert a new line in my femoral artery.

'Where's that?' I asked.

'Here.' She pressed her index and middle fingers, hard, onto the inside of my upper thigh, catching a portion of my ball sack as she did so. I closed my eyes.

The ICU doctor used an ultrasound to guide a needle into my femoral artery. I spread my legs.

'Just a gentle prick,' she said.

But the thing was a big mother of a needle and she had to really jab it into the inside of my thigh. On the ultrasound screen I saw the needle slide into a throbbing artery. She stitched it in place and with a dry look told me to try lying still. And then she faded back into the Fraternity.

In the late afternoon the leeches arrived, in pairs, like lovers.

'What are they for?' asked Lisa sharply.

Quan and Michael looked away.

'Are they really going to use leeches?'

My parents nodded.

'They will suck the blood out of the fingers,' Dad explained.

Despite the medical advances of the last millennium, it is still nature's marvel, the humble hermaphroditic leech, that is the finest bloodletting agent in modern medicine. As the leech bites, it injects a blood-thinning anticoagulant, an anaesthetic, and it's voracious! Leeching is called biotherapy in today's medical parlance, but when humankind first used leeches, in Egypt three and a half thousand years ago, it was called 'leeching'. Leeches were popular for bloodletting in the nineteenth century, but by 1900 their medical potential was discredited, and they only appeared on children playing in tepid swamps. Then, in the 1980s, biotherapeutic leeching was used successfully with reconstructive surgery. And that's how a slither of leeches came to be sucking up against the side of a jar, next to my uneaten meatloaf, in the ICU.

Many of the Fraternity had not used leeches before, and there was some amusement at their appearance. They named the leeches: Posh and Becks, Brad and Angelina, Homer and Marge.

'What about superhero names?' I suggested.

'No,' the Fraternity moaned, 'too boring.'

The leeches had been reared in Liverpool, on a leech farm, and, after their tour of duty on me, they would go back there, fat and happy, to be sterilised. The lives of medical leeches follow sumptuous highs with toxic lows.

I watched the mouths of Simon and Garfunkel suck up against the side of the jar, their pointy tails flailing in space. A look of horror crossed Lisa's face, followed by a veil of white.

Quan had some leeching experience. He closed my curtain and cut a hole in the bottom of a paper cup, which he then slipped over my thumb and sealed with tape. 'We don't want the leeches escaping and getting into your bandages.'

My skinned thumb dripped blue blood onto the cup's sides. Quan squirted a sugar solution called dextran onto my thumb; the leeches liked the taste of that. He unscrewed a jar and, between his index finger and thumb, pulled out Sonny. Big Sonny tried to curl himself around Quan's thumb but was quickly dropped into the paper cup. Quan covered the open end of the cup with cling film. Sonny unwound and sampled my blood pooling on the bottom of the cup. And then, tentatively, almost as if he was ashamed at the riches before him, Big Sonny snatched onto the side of my thumb and began to pulsate.

I felt calm. Really, I didn't mind them. They were less repulsive than, say, maggots.

Then Quan left. The Fraternity popped a head through my curtain to say that my brother and sister, Richard and Sarah, were waiting to see me. Richard was leaving for Melbourne in a few hours. He was moving there for good and I was keen to see him. But my nurse said that he needed to fix four more leeches to my un-leeched fingers, and that Richard and Sarah would have to wait.

This nurse of mine had never used leeches. My impression of his attitude was perhaps blighted by ketamine and morphine, but, to me, he seemed excited. Something in his manner suggested morbid fascination and authoritarianism. I loathed it.

He set about affixing the leeches with a painfully bull-headed slowness. Unlike how Sonny Boy had been with Quan, the leeches with the nurse were reluctant, recalcitrant and showed no respect, and they refused the succulent dextran with which he swabbed my fingers. The nurse's bearded jaw set itself in a determined, stubborn clench. His neck tensed. His face reddened. He cajoled, swore at, tenderly stroked and aggressively squeezed Cher, Charlie and Chaplin, until they finally latched onto my index, middle and ring fingers. By then it was 6 p.m.

'One more to go,' said the nurse, a trickle of sweat rolling over the ridge of his brow, across his hollow cheek, and into his spindly beard.

'Maybe give it a break for a minute,' I said, hopefully.

'No!'

It took him an hour to get Posh onto my bloated pinky. I sighed at his unbending stubbornness. At the peak of the frustration, while his lips were pulled back over his teeth in a sneer, I asked, 'Mate, can we finish up here?'

'In a minute,' he spat through clenched teeth.

It took him ten more minutes to get Posh suckling on my pinky.

'There!' he said defiantly.

Richard came in. He was tight up against his airport schedule. He managed a smile. I was in the kind of situation that would really get to him: all laid up and leeched to the shithouse. I wanted to say that I would miss him, and that I was proud of him, but, I don't know, I just wished him luck, and he wished me luck, and we said goodbye for a long while.

Sarah, her husband, Rob, and their baby, Chester, were also in the waiting room. They came in and Sarah stayed for a while. She sat with me a lot while I was in intensive care. When Lisa needed a break, or my parents needed a break, Sarah was there. In silent moments, when I felt like I was going to have to tell her that I didn't want to talk, she'd say, 'You don't have to talk, just go to sleep.'

'Does Luke know?' I asked Sarah.

It was important to me that he knew. I believed that he would understand what it had been like in the water, and I wanted someone to understand it. He knew how it was to surf on an afternoon like that, in conditions like that; we'd done it together countless times. I wanted to know if I'd done the wrong thing. I'm not sure why it was so important to find someone to ask about this, but as I lay in the ICU it seemed crucial to me. Sarah said she would get in touch with Luke and let him know what had happened.

In the evening a nurse called Anju came on shift. She was in her mid-twenties, with dark eyes, dark hair and dense, shapely eyebrows. Her eyes widened when the Fraternity showed her the leeches. She didn't complain, though, only a deep sigh escaped her. She raised her eyebrows, and we laughed together.

When the leeches fell off my fingers, Anju put their plump, blood-drunk bodies into jars of salt water. She shook them until the water turned red with leech vomit. That was called purging. A leech can survive for weeks on a gutful of blood, but the Fraternity wanted them hungry. Once they were purged, they could be re-used. What a critter!

Anju lined up five paper cups and tried to affix George Jetson to my thumb, without any success. We discussed the flawed leech-attachment procedure: dropping leeches into a cup and begging them to attach was ridiculous. Leeches don't respond to begging, or insults, they can't be reasoned with, and if you drop them in a paper cup, then most times they don't know what the fuck to do.

I asked Dad for help. He came in and cut the end off a large plastic syringe and put George Jetson inside. Using the stopper he pushed the leech down the syringe until its only exit was onto a tasty digit. Dad got the Jetsons attached in fifteen minutes and it was an absolute relief compared to the previous hours of swearing and frustration.

It got late and visiting hours ended. The ICU quietened down. TVs were on, curtains were drawn, machines beeped rhythmically, dinner came. Anju drew 300 millilitres of blood from my hand. She suctioned another 300 out of my bed. My heparin rate was 14 millilitres an hour, up from 9 an hour. I was really bleeding. I was tired and about to press the morphine button when I got dizzy.

'I don't feel right,' I told her.

She looked at the monitors.

The room blurred. I lost my breath. An alarm rang.

'Doctor!' yelled Anju.

The Fraternity scrambled. From their multitude popped a young Englishman with a strong accent, curly hair and a white coat. He whipped my curtain open. Nurses gathered. A thick mattress of exhaustion lay on me and I couldn't move. My eyes darted from face to face. The young doctor gave orders.

'Turn that down.' He pointed at a drip. 'Turn that up.'

I watched his face, while the Fraternity watched me. I was aware of their interest and, vaguely, of noises, of fast-moving fingers, of sirens. I sank into the mattress: it folded over and buried me.

'How do you feel?' asked the doctor.

I said nothing.

Anju did something frantically. My eyes closed, and I could not open them.

This is bad.

I was in the water flailing, not moving.

I might die now.

Then I began to wake, as if from sluggish sleep. I felt a sickening nausea, but I could move, and I saw the lights on the ceiling, and the mattress lifted off me.

'How do you feel now?' the doctor asked.

'Better,' I croaked.

The doctor watched the monitors as my dizziness steadied and the nausea ebbed away.

'You feel better?'

'What happened?' I asked weakly.

'You had a hypotensive episode.'

I'd been bleeding too fast, so the doctor had shut off my heparin, increased my blood transfusion volume, and filled me up.

Of everything that I had experienced in the ICU – sleep deprivation, shark nightmares, hallucinations, leeches – it was this hypotensive episode that frightened me the most. The fear of a quiet death. I'd seen trolleys being raced through the ICU, and seen the way the nurses and the Fraternity turned to watch them going past. I'd listened to the yelling and clanking, but it had been impossible to discern the results – someone may have just slipped away, no family with them, maybe not even conscious, they may have just slipped into a void. I didn't want to fall away and end life without a sound, too weak to help myself. I'd felt as close to death in those moments as I had in the ocean. I was sure this doctor had saved my life.

'That's my job,' he said.

My heart hammered. The doctor reassured me that my bleeding was controlled, that everything was being done to save my hand. I'd had it, though. Shaken up, I became erratic. Anju gave me some drugs to calm me down.

The Fraternity called in Michael, the Plastics registrar. He sewed up something in my forearm to slow the bleeding. He talked to me calmly and his tone was relaxed; he spoke about his exams and the apprenticeship that doctors go through to become Plastics. He lived in a one-bedroom apartment five minutes from the hospital, worked fourteen-hour days, was on call at night, and had little time for a life outside medicine. Basically, the hospital was his life. Michael told Anju to give me a bag of blood every hour and said that I could get the Fraternity to call him at any hour and he would come.

Anju affixed a new leech. She accidentally squirted my blood on her face, and it dribbled down her cheek.

'I don't have anything,' I blurted out.

She wiped her face. 'I know,' she said.

As I slept, I dreamt of the ocean; of floating on a mirrored sea, unable to see below me, but knowing the shark was there. I rolled into a foetal position on my surfboard.

I woke with Michael standing over me.

'What happened?' I asked him.

He looked worried.

'You had another hypotensive episode.'

I'd been unconscious this time and missed the excitement. Anju was already stringing up new bags of blood above me. Michael stopped the heparin, and the leeches. I was sedated while he sutured up whatever he could find that was bleeding in my arm, and something down deep in me said, *Fuck the hand.*

I wanted that thought to stop. I told myself to put up a fight, that there were only eight days left.

FUCK the hand.

I drifted in and out of a ketamine nightmare.

That day, I was given 12 units of red cells, 2 units of plasma, 2 of platelets, and several litres of intravenous saline. The bags of blood that had gone into me in the morning had bled out by 2 a.m.

DAY
PLUS
5

A new nurse opened my curtain. She saw the leeches. She'd seen every colour of shit and spew but drew the line at leeches, so she asked if she could change shifts. I understood. Some people freak out about heights, or public toilets – for her it was biotherapeutic leeches. So Colleen, a slim Pommy girl with an easygoing personality, took my shift instead. She held out a bedpan and wanted me to fill it, but I sent it back empty. She looked at the Fraternity, and then at me.

'Are you in pain?'

'No,' I muttered.

I saw this kid get constipated at school camp one time; he took slow steps and I heard him crying sometimes. I was eleven, and I thought he was a pussy.

Colleen slid the bedpan back under me.

'Keep trying.'

I didn't want it. I had things on my mind: I had seven days left to see if my hand would live, and a baby due in about four and a half months. And fate chose that moment, with the bedpan still under me, for Quan, Michael and the Fraternity to arrive to rewrap my bandages. I stared at the ceiling.

We have a baby coming.

Get out of here.

My bandages were caked with blood, some crusty, some coagulated and some glistening. Michael peeled them off and my forearm flopped open like a badly folded calzone. They hadn't sewed it shut yet. I saw inside a part of myself that I'd hoped not to see again, and it was mushy, grey and shapeless, defined by a line of shark tooth-serrated skin.

Michael put his gloved fingers inside my arm. I didn't feel pain, because there are no pain nerves that deep. He re-bandaged it and the Fraternity checked the leeches on my fingers. Then they all went beyond my curtain to talk business, and Colleen surreptitiously slid the empty bedpan out from under me. Just then, Lisa and my parents came in.

'Good morning,' they said.

My voice shook in reply.

'Are you okay?' asked Lisa.

'It's not an arm.'

Then I started with some short breaths.

'I was attacked by a shark,' I told Dad.

Then came unwanted tears, and while one part of me lay stiff, disgusted, and thinking how weak I was, the rest of me covered my face with my right hand. The Fraternity saw me break down and a sentence was scribbled in my medical notes that ended with the word 'psychiatrist'. I pressed my fingers into my eyes and Lisa pulled my hand away. I was trapped inside a person that was not me. I counted aloud, trying to settle down. I felt the ICU listening. I sensed the pan man next to me fall silent. Dad talked quietly and he spoke to me for a long time, and, when I'd calmed down, I told him about the blood pressure crashes.

'Fuck the hand,' I said.

Lisa thought I was at an absolute low, that I was being irrational.

She asked Kevin Ho to talk to me. Twenty minutes later he came through my curtain.

'I promise you, mate, you won't leave like this. You will leave intact,' he said. 'I need to leave your arm open to give your hand the best chance of survival.'

He asked me to think about my arm as an object, an abstract concept. 'For now, your arm isn't your arm,' he said. 'Can you live with that?'

Then Kevin stopped the ketamine and took away the morphine button. He didn't say why, but I knew – my mental state had deteriorated. I could see it on their faces. I could hear it in their gentle questions and smiling encouragement.

Everyone left except Lisa.

'I'll never surf again,' I told her.

'Yes, I think you will.'

'Don't you want me to stop?'

'I don't know.'

'I would jump at every shadow. I would fear every moment.'

She nodded, but said, 'You don't know that.'

Lisa was physically drained, emotionally exhausted.

'You will overcome anything you really want to,' she told me.

Colleen held out the bedpan.

'I can't,' I said.

'You're in pain.'

She was right. The ketamine had been diluting most sensations of pain, but now it was gone and the dreadful state of my intestinal tract made its presence felt. Colleen talked about something called Microlax. She spoke in calming tones, so that the word 'enema' skipped by unobtrusively amid other words like 'common', 'nothing to be embarrassed about', 'loosen' and 'relief'.

I said, 'No way.'

She gave me peppermint tea, which exploded into gas inside me. I relented to the Microlax, and after it Colleen checked the bedpan like she was counting change, and her smile was lopsided but encouraging. Regardless of this mediocre event, though, it wasn't long before painful rumbles began inside me again.

Colleen gave me eight bags of blood. The Fraternity wrote a note, under 'Issues', referring to this as a 'massive' transfusion.

Jane, the head ICU nurse, came on shift later that evening. She had no problem with the leeches – she had the kind of fortitude needed to drench sheep and butcher deer. There was not even a wafer of disgust in her voice as she applied those recalcitrant leeches.

'Come on, baby,' she'd say. 'Get on there.'

Jane was particularly concerned about the leeches escaping in the ICU. If one escaped into my bandages and attached itself to an exposed artery, well, that would be a poor outcome for me; but if it got loose in the ICU, the whole place would be compromised. When Jane found a leech missing, the Fraternity would go to battle stations. They usually found the leech in my bed, satiated and sleeping, or attached to a buttock cheek. However, on one occasion, after a scramble through my bedding, an escaping leech was seen arching its way across the ICU linoleum. Jane pounced on that leech and quarantined it in a jar marked for death. A sad end.

Late in the night I was in serious pain.

Look at this jumble of a life.

Sleep was impossible. I was at the end of the stretched bit of my tether. I refused further laxatives and enemas. I begged Jane for a real, porcelain toilet.

'I *need* gravity.'

Jane spoke to the Fraternity, and a few minutes later she rolled in a toilet seat on wheels called a 'commode'. I pressed my bed's remote control button until I was in a sitting position.

Oh, commode!

Sometimes I know exactly what I am capable of, what my body can do, and I knew I needed that commode. Jane called in an orderly.

'We are going to get you on your feet, okay?'

'Shit, yes,' I said.

Jane unplugged my heart monitors. An alarm went off. The guy next to me, the pan man, moaned. Jane lowered my bed, swung my legs to the side, and sat me up slowly. The orderly helped me to my feet, while I held my tubes bundled in my good hand. I was nearly naked, having on only a pair of pyjama pants with a catheter snaking through the fly. The orderly held me up.

'I'm okay,' I said.

The orderly let go. I stood without support. I smiled. I was thinking of the shark, and I thought, *Fuck you.*

On the ICU linoleum, I stood on my own for the first time since the attack. I felt strong for the first time.

I am on my own two feet, you bastard.

Stu came to mind, his battle with cancer, and thinking of him inspired me.

I'm going to give this a massive crack. I am going to save this hand.

Jane helped me onto the commode. She put a buzzer in my hand and told me to ring when I needed her. Then she closed the curtain, her footseps shuffled just a few feet away, and she waited. The humiliating, unanticiated and painful bowel suffering ended then.

Commode – what a precious invention.

When Jane had got me back into bed, I was shaking.

'I'm going to save my hand,' I told her.

I started babbling. Her eyes were on my monitors. I got cold.

She piled blankets on me. The shaking became uncontrollable.

'What's wrong?' I asked.

'You're upset. Calm down.'

The shaking kept on for a time. My jaw clenched.

My own two feet.

My own two feet.

DAY
PLUS
6

At midnight I woke up. Jane said that all the leeches had been used at least once, so she'd started using recycled ones and they took longer to attach. They sulked in the corner of the paper cups. It took an hour to get them on. I drifted into tiring little sleeps between leeching and observations and leeching. At 7 a.m., when Colleen came back on duty, I was listless and beaten.

Colleen told me she could take my catheter out, if I liked.

If I like?

She said that I would have to pass 300 millilitres of urine within two hours, or the Fraternity would want the catheter back in.

'No problem.'

She said it wouldn't hurt taking it out. 'Lie back and relax.'

She reached under my sheet and pulled the catheter out of me – it was a long bit of piping and it came out with a whoosh. My lips puckered into a flower and I drew in air that whistled over my teeth. It was weird, but, in a painful way, it also felt good. I quickly passed a quart of the required specimen, and gave the Fraternity no opportunity to get their catheter back in.

The minor downside was that in order to urinate, I had to ask for a bottle, and every time I took a piss the nurse would hold my bottle up to the light, like a jeweller would a diamond, examining it for luminescence, colour, quality and size. It was humiliating to have my piss described as poor or unsatisfactory in some way.

'Bottle, please,' moaned the pan man next to me. 'Get us a bottle!' he yelled.

His nurse tripped over herself getting him a clean bottle from the storeroom. There was something about the way the pan man groaned for a bottle that stirred a feeling in me.

'Can I have a bottle, please?' I asked, and Colleen dashed to the storeroom.

And in tandem like that, all day, every twenty minutes, the pan man and I caused a tangle of Fraternity inside that bottle room. And all day they recycled leeches on me. My dad came in to help. He had the knack of getting those leeches on. I helped too. I lost myself in the process: attach, detach, purge, prepare. The leeches were getting weary – attaching for a half-hour spell and then rolling up catatonically.

I looked out the window at a night that had arrived quickly. My bleeding had slowed. They didn't put a drop of blood in me all day. My hand looked good: pink fingers, good blood flow. Five days to go.

DAY
PLUS
7

Early in the morning, Colleen rolled an armchair into my curtained area, and after ten minutes of physical exertion, and tube disentanglements, I was sitting upright. The ICU looked inexplicably different from a vertical plane. For the first time I could visualise walking across it. I felt 10 per cent more human.

The leeches had stopped attaching by then. They had all been used at least twice, and they were over it. There were no more leeches. I'd bled them dry. By midday the leech therapy was over. Kevin Ho said the hand looked good. There was great hope. I was becoming a person again. I would have my hand.

At noon a pregnant physiotherapist jovially introduced herself. Lisa talked with her about the actual process of giving birth, and they both laughed nervously. I got on my feet. I was wobbly, but I managed five squats and a few leg lifts. It was good for Lisa to see me do that. My weakest days had passed. The physio brought over an exercise bike. I rode 5 kilometres.

Colleen gave me Endone.

Colleen gave me oxycodone.

Colleen gave me gabapentin.

I don't remember the rest.

Lisa needed a break, so Mum stayed with me in the ICU. I rested easily in her presence. She was very calm, and watchful, and not a stranger to tough times. She believed strongly in various philosophies, and one in particular: 'Don't let the bastards get you down.'

That was her main one – defiance. I really admired that.

My arm ached intensely. I asked for the exercise bike and cycled for twenty-five minutes. It took my mind off the pain until analgesic flattened me. I dozed off with two bags of blood flowing into me.

Four days to go.

DAY PLUS 11

My fever was just starting when Damo and Mud came to visit me, and I was groggy. I saw them in a blur. On their minds was the horror of the shark.

'Did you see it, mate?'

'No,' I said.

They stayed a while. We talked of things I don't recall, but I clearly felt the gears of our friendship mesh and glide. And, from my sunken doze, I felt myself rising up through the fever to be with them. *My good friends. These are my good friends.*

Damo and I had planned to meet the night of the attack.

'I don't want you think that this was your fault,' I told him.

He looked at the ground, and he looked at me, and I could see it was something that had bothered him.

'Thanks, mate,' he said.

'Don't be stupid,' I said.

My friends left smiling.

The fever turned into a horrible draining thing. The Fraternity didn't like that there was an infection somewhere. They injected antibiotics. I lay still. There was no freedom; hoses all over me. The entire place was a trap. The exterior world imploded into nothing. My will grew thin. I felt lost in time and as if the days in ICU were dripping by; bulbous droplets that grew, and fell, and endlessly returned.

Lisa's exhaustion mirrored mine. She had deteriorated without me seeing it. Dad told me, 'You tell her to go home, mate. She is here from dawn to dusk. She's not eating dinner until 10 o'clock. It's not good for her.'

I asked Lisa to go home earlier. It was a robotic sentence, as my selfishness wanted her to stay. She was quiet and she didn't argue. She tried to smile, I tried to smile, and then she left. Dad and Mum stayed while I ate what little dinner I could. I left half-eaten mash, nibbled bread, and took a spoonful of pale custard from a bowl.

'Come on, mate. You need protein,' they said.

They watched me chew rubbery pieces of pasta.

My parents had been down to Bondi Beach, and walked on the wet sand near the water. They said it was blustery and choppy in the water, and the beach was empty of people, but there were surfers out.

'Thirty surfers,' Dad said.

They counted how many waves broke out the back and came all the way to shore.

'Hardly any.'

Later, they headed home, and Mum went into the shower and cried.

I watched Kevin looking at my fingers. The bleeding from the thumb was a bit sluggish, but acceptable.

'Just look at that, mate,' he said. 'The natural curl of the fingers is exactly right.'

The skin was purple and bloated, the hand was like a fat octopus, but the fingers did curl gently at the knuckles. He had stitched the tendons up perfectly.

'I know you're having some bad days, Glenn, but this hand is looking good.'

He smiled and it had become night so he left. I asked the nurse to shut my curtain, because the pain came hard in the evenings. The Fraternity called the pain 'phantom limb pain', but it was no phantom to me; it was electricity down my arm and an ache as big as a log on my elbow. The Fraternity told me that morphine wasn't addictive if I was in pain, but I felt like I was using too much of it.

My hand had survived for eight full days; it only needed to survive one more day to make it to the morning of the tenth day. And on that penultimate day, a thug – fever – came early in the dark hours after midnight. It dragged me into haze and began to suffocate me. It frustrated the Fraternity, it annoyed the Plastics, and I could not bear it. They all said it was the open wound. Michael was sent to find the infection. He dug around in my arm. Battered nerves shrieked at me.

What is he doing!

Michael unwound the outer bandages.

This is the last thing I need right now, said the nerves.

Michael pulled off gauze that was blood-glued to the wound.

Are you joking? my nerves screamed, and the sound of it in my head came into my throat as a groan I tried to suppress.

'You okay?' asked Michael.

My arm gaped, and its serrated edges roared as it folded open.

Michael found no infection. He sighed.

'It might be the CVC line.'

He pulled out the CVC line. It wasn't infected. My temperature stayed above 39 degrees.

'Give him blood,' said Michael.

My temperature dropped to 37.

Michael didn't tell me that he had found a 1-centimetre section of flesh in my palm that was necrotic: black and dead. That was the furthest up that dead tissue had been found.

When dawn arrived, I noticed that my mobile phone was in a bag next to my chair. I turned it on. The message bank was full. I dropped it away. On the roof was a yellowed ceiling fan that trundled around looking sick.

Lisa came in with the two French surfers, Mikael and Sebastian. Mikael gave me the legrope he had used as a tourniquet. He showed me how he did it. He knew where the artery was. It is very difficult to convey to someone who has saved your life how much you think of them. I tried for words, and stumbled, and looked at Lisa; she knew I was drug-addled, and her face told me that it didn't matter. I told them that I was happy. I meant much more, though. They left, and I thought that they were so capable, so young.

Kevin Ho rang me.

'I'm here with a marine biologist, Vic Peddemors, from the Department of Primary Industries. He has been looking at pre-surgery photos of your arm, and he knows what kind of shark it was.' Kevin hesitated. 'Are you up to hearing this?'

'I'm fine.'

'Okay, I'll put him on.'

Vic Peddemors had a South African accent, which struck me as sensible and trustworthy.

'It was a 2.5-metre great white,' he said. 'A great white of that size is considered a juvenile, but is on the verge of adulthood. Its diet is changing from fish to mammals. I think this shark was testing new prey.'

'Why didn't it come back?' I asked.

'It didn't like you, basically. Great whites are known for taking a test bite, and if they don't like it, they let go. To be honest, you were lucky it was a great white. If I had to be bitten by a shark, I'd want it to be a great white.'

'Is there something about me, about the way I paddle or something, and that's why it came for me?'

'No. You just . . . You were separated from the crowd. It wasn't anything else.'

'That's good . . . I don't know if I'll ever be able to go in the ocean again. It's meant a lot to me —'

'Listen, mate, I've spoken to a lot of shark victims, and there are two types: those who want to forget everything, and those who need to know everything. You sound like the second type. When you leave hospital, give me a call, I'll tell you about sharks.'

The Department of Primary Industries was obliged to release Vic's findings to the media. The hospital was expecting headlines. Kevin's staff were already fielding media calls nonstop, as was the St Vincent's PR baron. He wanted me to consider a press conference, but I knew Lisa wouldn't accept that, no way. I picked up my mobile phone. I wasn't supposed to use it in the ICU, but I rang Lisa anyway. I told her it was a great white and I heard her swallow.

'Okay?' I asked.

'How do you feel?'

'Fine. The attack was just a freak event. I'd started thinking that it was my fault, somehow.'

I breathed in.

'The hospital wants me to do a press conference,' I went on.

'No way.'

'It will shut everyone up —'

'*No*, you're in no condition for a press conference. Just tell them no. You are sick. The press just want all the gory details.'

'It's the best way to —'

'It's none of their business!'

'We should at least release a statement . . .'

'No.'

'Yeah.'

'I'm coming in.'

'No, don't. Let me make a call. I'll ring you back.'

I rang a friend who was an editor at a major newspaper. He promised to draft up a media release that would give the story but keep personal details and shark horrors to a minimum. I knew that Lisa would take some convincing, she was so protective, but I felt like I knew what to do.

On that night of my ninth day with my hand on, there was footage of great whites on the news, big mothers eating meat. 'Great White at Bondi' was the headline. I watched it on my TV with the curtain open and the sound down. It was on the other TVs as well. The Fraternity watched, and I felt some patients look my way. I lay still. The pan man had his curtain shut. I looked at Matt, the Crohn's sufferer, but he was in a fast and peaceful-looking sleep. I closed my eyes.

The Fraternity checked my fingers. The thumb had got itself bleeding well again. I really didn't understand why it was so fickle.

Just bleed, you little bastard.

The bleeding from the pinky and ring fingers had slowed.

The bleeding, I realised, was just the way it was – ups and downs, swings and roundabouts – the rollercoaster of the ICU.

I made it to the morning of day ten with my hand on. Ten days: it was the magic day, and this was it – surely this was it now. The hand would make it.

Jane, the head nurse, opened my curtain and told me I was being discharged from the ICU that afternoon. She was smiling.

I stood for a few minutes and felt strength in me. I smiled and made jokes with the Fraternity. I rode thirty minutes on the exercise bike at a good clip.

'I've got a surprise for you,' said Jane.

She put me in a wheelchair and pushed me through the ICU's hydraulic doors. It felt colder outside them, like there was less air out there. An elevator, made wide for wheelchairs, took me down five floors to the hospital lobby, which bustled with sick and healthy people, employees and tradesmen, a gift shop, a florist, and a cafe in the corner looking over a small park. I was dressed inconspicuously in pyjamas and a hospital gown and bandages. Most people crossing the lobby didn't notice me, and those who did looked down on me with smiles and I smiled back. Jane wheeled me up to a window in the cafe where the sun streamed onto the table and glinted on the cutlery, and then Lisa arrived and sat down happily.

With my left arm slung across my waist, my hand wrapped in discoloured bandages, I stared out at the real world and recognised it again. Lisa held my right hand across the table.

'Like old times,' she said.

I held my face up to the sun. And instead of tears in her eyes, there came a grin and she said, 'We are the lucky ones.'

'I know.'

I ordered a burger and a berry smoothie, but was so exhausted halfway through lunch that Jane had to come and take me back to bed.

Lisa eventually agreed to me giving a media release, as a necessary evil, so long as it was written well – no gory horror show. She brought some photos in that I had asked her for. In the photos, I was next to other family members, so Lisa cut me out in the shape of a person. Kevin Ho read the press release and scratched out a few words.

'This is a bit too personal,' he said. 'Put it in a book one day.'

He took the photos, as it was planned that Kevin and the Director of Surgery would give a press conference and release my statement the next day.

'It's been ten days.' Kevin smiled.

He told me he could rebuild my forearm by taking muscle from my inner thigh to replace the muscle I had lost to the shark.

'Saving the hand is only step one,' he added.

To get it moving, and feeling, was going to be a long, painful journey that would take years. The Fraternity came in while he unwrapped my hand. The pinky finger had stopped bleeding and looked a blacker shade of purple. Kevin grimaced.

'The fingers look great. The thumb is bleeding slowly, but is fine. Your pinky is heavily congested, although I think it is still viable,' he said.

He told the Fraternity to make sure the hand stayed warm. He insisted that they keep the Bair Hugger on me at all times. Everything was viable.

Ten days gone.

I was readied to leave the ICU.

Then my temperature spiked to 39 degrees, and the Fraternity cancelled the move, and I stayed in the ICU.

DAY
PLUS
17

After my fever broke I was again readied to move out of the ICU. The Fraternity wanted me showered first, so Colleen, the nice English nurse, wrapped my left arm in a plastic bag, stripped me, and sat me on a plastic chair in the ICU shower cubicle. She turned the water on and shut the door. I sat bent over, elbow on knee, and let warm water flatten my hair, run against my neck and tip over my shoulders. It was all I heard: the shower drain, clear water pouring off my face onto tiles. I breathed through the torrent, and felt water run down my sides. It was a brief moment when I didn't have any worries.

Just before I was to leave the ICU, the PR dude came to see me. The media was downstairs for the press conference.

'Wouldn't you like to say a few words?'

I said no. He left.

The Fraternity removed my arterial cannula, and they took the heart monitors off, and the calf compressors – a lot of tubes just disappeared, leaving me with just one cannula in my arm. I thanked the Fraternity and the nurses. The pan man had already gone, but I waved to Matt and his girlfriend, Grace.

Downstairs, at the press conference, Kevin explained Paul de Gelder's injuries and my injuries: the two shark guys. He called us men of high mental fortitude, and he said he was hopeful of my hand reattaching. The media reported that I could move my fingers. I got a lot of email congratulations about that, but it wasn't true.

I was moved to a ward room and Lisa was waiting there when I was rolled in. She brought in the cards and flowers she'd been storing (the Fraternity hadn't wanted that stuff cluttering up the ICU), and the room filled with colour. My schoolmates had signed a card with a photo of our rugby team in it – Luke had signed that one. My nanna sent a card, and my uncles, Elizabeth too, and my uni mates. It was a lot to take in. Lisa and I enjoyed those moments reading the cards.

The ward room had a big window facing north-east, with a view of Paddington, Vaucluse, the harbour and Dover Heights behind. The sun came in, and I sat in a chair looking over the hills to the sea.

Kevin arrived to check my fingers. The blood from my thumb and pinky was dark, and that meant it was venous, deoxygenated blood trapped in the capillaries. The blood from my other fingers was bright red arterial blood. The hand had lived for eleven days. Kevin told me it all looked okay.

'We're not quite ready to pop the champagne,' he said, 'but you can buy the bottle.'

I asked him about Paul de Gelder, and he said that Paul had taken to hopping around the navy ward and wanted to lift weights. His example didn't leave me much scope to wallow. So when the physio asked me if I wanted to try to walk, I stumbled through two laps of the ward with Lisa and Mum watching on, my left arm supported by a trolley and my right hand dragging a metal pole on which my drip was hung.

My hand had been on for twelve days when my pinky finger died. The tips of the fingers were dead too. Kevin came in, looking very serious.

'I'm not going to bullshit you. You're going to lose your pinky.'

That was okay. I was okay with no pinky. It wasn't too bad an effort by the pinky: twelve days.

I slept really well that night. It was the first full night of sleep I'd had in hospital. And I didn't get a temperature, I didn't even dream, but I woke up thinking something was wrong.

In the morning the Plastics found that my index finger was dead. The tops of my middle and ring fingers were dead. Only my thumb and the lower joints of my middle and ring fingers were viable. I prayed for their recovery.

I've got to put up a fight.

Lisa and my parents wheeled me outside to the park. As we sat on a little bench, the sun shone on me. It was my birthday. I was thirty-four.

My brother Tim arrived. He'd left his campervan in Tasmania, where he had been on holiday, and brought his wife and three kids back to Sydney. It was important to me to have him there. He seems to know more about life and its meaning than anyone I know.

He sat with me in the ward room, and I talked about the night on the Ridgeway Road. I apologised. He only said that it was funny the things that stick with people all their lives.

Tim and Lisa were there the next morning when Kevin came in to look at the hand. The fingers were all dead. The thumb was dead. Kevin talked about making me a craw, so I could use my palm as a kind of tong. Lisa's eyes widened. When we were alone I told her, 'I don't want a craw.'

I fell into a mighty depression right then. I hadn't felt like that for a long while, but I fell into the hole in minutes. No tears, no sobs, just a black dog on me like a weight. *Why me?* got me.

My hand lived for thirteen bloody days.

My haemoglobin level plummeted. They gave me two units of blood. That didn't touch the sides of the trench I was in.

I told Lisa, 'I can't face this.' I had no more will. I told her I wanted it to end.

And then the psychiatrist was called, and he came to check I wasn't suicidal. People streamed in and out. Tim told them all to go away, and that he would deal with it. And he sat with me, and talked, and the sound of his voice and the way he talked got the weight shifting.

'You will keep the hand,' he said.

I liked that. The calm of his presence washed over me. But I knew he was wrong about the hand. The fight was over. My hand was dead. And as he went on, the certainty of my situation came into focus, and I felt better. I finally knew the outcome. I was at the end. No more could be, or could have been, done. The problem had a solution. There was a relief in that. I told Tim that I was okay, and I found that I meant it.

After a while, Kevin returned, and he didn't mention the craw again, because the entire hand was dead and there could be no craw. It had deteriorated very quickly. He wanted to amputate on Sunday. I would get the Saturday to rest. I spent that Saturday outside with Lisa and my parents, and Tim and his family, and with Sarah and her family. It was a good day.

On amputation day, everyone waited in the ward with me at 7.30 a.m. No one knew what to say and there was nothing to say. At 9 o'clock I was prepared for surgery. During a moment to myself, I unwrapped my hand. It was black and cold, like ashes. It wasn't a hand. I was going to have it cut off, but it was already gone.

While I was in surgery Lisa talked to my dad as our mothers whispered together. They had grown closer. That was one good thing.

Kevin Ho sawed through the bone 4 centimetres back from my wrist. That got him sweating. He said it was damn thick bone. He pulled skin over the end of the bone and sewed it up. He took skin off my thigh and grafted it over the medial part of my forearm so that it could be closed up. Kevin saved most of my forearm. He was a very good surgeon.

I woke in the ward feeling confused. I asked Lisa where my hand was. I asked why the shark didn't come back. As the drugs wore off, the confusion faded and by the afternoon I felt good. When my family left that night, I felt like my old self, even though I wasn't. I felt like I would sleep well. I felt that I was lucky.

DAY
PLUS
22

It seemed like there was nothing more to worry about. There was no more bleeding, no fever, and there wasn't much for me to do. So I just rested and watched daytime TV. This was the melancholy killer: nothing to do. I lapped the ward, trailing my drip. The other patients wondered who I was as I kept coming around witnessing their convalescence. Who was I, shuffling past the dividing line between their happy days and sad? Who was I, interrupting their daytime TV?

The Plastics visited me regularly. They unwrapped and rewrapped my various bandages, and along with that came the requisite peeling and grizzle and gritted teeth. My skin grafts were going well, and Kevin went away on a well-deserved, shark victim-free holiday. I just saw the Plastics every once in a while.

I remained in hospital solely for wound dressing and pain management. Mentally, I was already elsewhere. I was over the four-hourly observations. I wanted off rubber sheets. I was tired of the whole place. My mood fluctuated – I was happy sometimes, content to stare out the window, but also easily irritated.

Occasionally I snapped at Lisa; she didn't react to my tantrums and that made her an easy target. I'd kick myself about it afterwards, especially with her being pregnant and all. And I knew better, too, because I'd had one brief moment in the ocean when I'd understood that it was crucial to just love my wife really properly and that nothing else mattered. It had been a higher plane of understanding. But I found myself forgetting to be good to my wife when I was in shooting pain or stuck in the shower. An important spiritual lesson that had come to me – a very non-spiritual person – in the hardest seconds of my life, tended to disappear during the grind of the everyday.

One evening, I fell into a broken sleep and dreamt of being on that higher plane again, and living life right all the time. While I was half asleep, a nurse rolled me onto my side so she could sponge my back. And I thought, *Damn, don't sponge me when I'm on this higher plane.*

But she sponged me. And, after a thorough sponging, she wanted to roll me onto my back again, but I grunted, 'No, no.' She let me sleep on my side, and I'd forgotten that small comfort. I slept deeply, and I didn't wake throughout the night, and when I did wake I ate a fine meal. Then Lisa came in, and I smiled, and her face lit up.

Lisa put my arm into a sling and we went for a walk outside the hospital. We bought coffee, avoided smokers outside the hospital entrance, found a seat in some shade, and watched pedestrians going by. We spoke about how lovely it was to be outside, in the air, in the summer, with life intact.

Lisa reminded me that we'd sold our apartment, so we had househunting to do. I groaned inwardly. *Real life, already.* The word 'mortgage' appeared in the air (and in my mind, in white embossed 3D lettering) and while I watched it, I realised a weight had come onto me: financial worry. I looked up and watched the sky moving slowly. I thought about the baby coming.

I need to go back to work.

With a quiet smile Lisa told me that she was going out to dinner with her best friend Georgia that night. It was something normal for her, and a chance to put a distance between the last night she'd gone out, when everything had turned into a nightmare. I smiled. My beautiful wife had been my strength through terrible fears and I wanted this night out to be good for her.

But she had a difficult time at the dinner. It was hard for her to forget the hospital, and the horror, and she was pregnant and was quickly tired. She never said anything, but I knew she was still suffering from the stress and was worried about the baby.

That same night, in my room, I could not concentrate. I had been given books and DVDs and puzzles, but I couldn't do anything with them. I was so dosed on morphine and nerve drugs that my attention span was severely limited. There was, however, some material that was short enough for me to focus on: the newsletter of the Amputee Association of New South Wales. I didn't consider myself an 'amputee', but I was, so I got the pamphlet. That's what happens when one is an amputee even if they don't want to be.

The newsletter was full of the word 'stump'. I read this and was dispirited by its overuse. I mean, that is an unsavoury word. A stump is a useless thing. It's dead wood in the backyard – something that is in the way. And it is the kind of thing that I'd just want to dig up and fucking burn. A stump is the kind of thing that I'd pity someone else for having. I couldn't envisage what my arm stump would look like – a horrible mess, something to be pitied? I didn't want that. And I knew that if I called my arm a stump I'd never like it; I'd never consider it a part of me. I'd always be embarrassed by it and hate it. I didn't want to live like that.

Just before I left hospital, I received an email from Stu. 'I'm in remission,' he wrote. 'Big relief.'

I read that a few times.

Stu had a flair for understatement and in two short, grammatically dubious sentences he'd claimed his life again. I typed up several versions of a message I never sent, explaining how moved I was by what he'd achieved, but I was left without words and never sent anything. I knew I couldn't tell him he was an inspiration, because he'd just say, 'Aw, shucks.'

Six days past the amputation, I was discharged. I'd been in St Vincent's for twenty-two days, used 20 litres of blood, lost a few kilograms, lost a hand, but felt full up with happiness. I left at midday dressed in pyjama shorts and a white singlet, and with a blue sling on my arm that held my elbow at 90 degrees. Lisa was given a bag full of medication for me: oxycodone, gabapentin and amitriptyline (an antidepressant). I took one of each before we left and my face drooped into a happy frown. I scored my pain zero out of ten.

I garbled goodbye to the hospital staff. It seemed like less of a goodbye than it deserved to be, but they were busy and had jobs to do and other people to save, and that was how it was. I floated past them all, through the hydraulic doors, and past the shining city view and the faces in the lobby, while leaning on Lisa and smiling insanely. It was a beautiful day outside; warm and breezeless, and dopey, kind of.

DAY
PLUS
29

Dad drove Lisa, Mum and me to Lisa's parents' house in Dover Heights. We all had dinner, and there was champagne. Lisa said, 'I don't think you should be drinking.'

'I'll be right.'

'You're on a lot of drugs, Glenn. I *really* don't think you should be drinking.'

'I'll just have a glass. One glass.'

All eyes turned to my dad, the doctor. He shrugged.

'Half a glass,' he said.

We clinked. I had three sips, then my eyes rolled up to the top of my head, and I said good night as I felt pain crawl into my arm. I dry-swallowed an amitriptyline tablet. It shoved me into a frozen sleep.

I woke in pitch blackness.

This is not the hospital.

I was lying in the same position I'd fallen asleep in, splayed on my back. My left arm tingled with pins and needles; I thought

I must have slept on it, but it was high up on a stack of pillows. I ran my right arm across the bed, and it was empty. I called out to Lisa, but the call sounded like only a voice in my head, and nothing came back. I lay awake waiting for her.

Lisa had woken earlier in the night. I'd taken up the majority of the foldout bed and pushed her to the edge. She was afraid that her movements might cause me pain so she crept out of the room. In the living room she encountered my mum standing in the dark.

'Jan?'

Mum looked at Lisa like she was a stranger.

'I'm looking for Glenn,' she said.

And from the sound of her voice, and the look on her face, Lisa knew that she was asleep.

'It's okay,' said Lisa.

She hugged her, and told her that everyone was safe, and walked her back to bed.

The next morning, as a grey light edged around the curtain, I felt my missing hand tighten into an uncomfortable fist and send flashes up my arm that stabbed me and rose to a terrible pitch. I breathed in and waited for the pain to abate, but it stayed. I scrabbled for the medication on the table, knocking the pills to the floor, and then had to get up and hold my arm like it was a baby. I shuffled out of the bedroom. Lisa was curled up on the couch.

'Is it your arm?' she asked.

'Yeah.'

I squeezed it to stop the flashing, but it didn't stop. Lisa looked uncomfortable.

She's pregnant.

'Come back to bed?' I asked.

I lay back down with my left arm held still against me, and

I tried not to squirm. Lisa gave me drugs, and after a while they leaned on my face and my expression pointed downwards and slackened. The flames in my arm died down, but they did not go away entirely. A baseline of inescapable pain lived in there now. I gave that baseline pain a four out of ten rating, like a shard of glass inside me that moved when I moved. I fell asleep wondering if it would be there forever.

I spent my days managing the pain, playing it off against sedation, trying to find the optimal mix – a mix that would let me talk and read but keep the pain below a five. Mornings were best; the activity that came with daylight, wrapping my arm and leg in plastic bags to shower in a plastic chair, discovering how to wash under my arms and dry my back, and eating, and the morning air – that was all good, that was okay. The house felt cool then, and full of food and music and the smell of tea-tree oil from the bathroom, and only a hush of traffic in the background. It was the afternoons that hurt, and the dusk. The pain spiked to sevens and nines in the dark. I hired an exercise bike and rode it in the late afternoons. It took a small part of my mind away from thinking about pain, but sometimes the only way to manage it was to drug myself senseless. I did that, and I told myself it would eventually go away. That would only be fair.

Every few days, with me well dosed on medication and gritting my teeth, Lisa drove me to the hospital. The driving was torture. The small vibrations of a moving car, the bumping that sends babies to sleep – more than ten minutes of that drove nails into my arm.

At St Vincent's, the Plastics reviewed my skin grafts, which were distasteful-looking, red and savage. I doubted they would ever turn to skin. But the Plastics rated them highly.

'Great granulation tissue,' they said.

They peeled off dying skin, and took out revealed stitches. It was unpleasant. The Plastics said my skin grafts would always look different to the rest of my arm.

No shit, I thought.

Along the wound, in a spiral pattern, were several identically sized white scars, all of them an inch long. They were the teeth marks.

Kevin told me that the pronator and supinator muscles in my forearm, which rotate the hand from palm up to palm down, were gone. Of the flexor and extensor muscles, which close and open the fist, the flexors were gone, but I still had some extensor muscles. Something still worked, anyway, because I was able to make small muscle movements in my forearm when I tried to move my now-nonexistent ring and pinky fingers.

'That's good,' said Kevin. 'It means you might be able to use a bionic hand.'

Kevin wanted me to start a rehab program, which meant: wound clinic, physiotherapy, occupational therapy, psychotherapy, pain clinic, prosthetic training, mirror therapy, and many other therapies. He gave me a referral to see Dr Greg Bowring, an upper-limb rehab specialist. I thanked Kevin; he had been really good to me.

Lisa drove me home through slow traffic. I held my slinged arm against my chest as it rang in pain, and I took a drug cocktail as soon as we got home.

DAY
PLUS
32

When I was alone, when Lisa was out and I was rattling around the house, I got started reading shark websites, and a question recurred:

Why me?

Of all the people. And of all beaches, Bondi. Of all the places I'd surfed, in all the murky dusks and uncrowded beach breaks, the shark got me at fucking Bondi. What were the chances of fate landing that lottery on me?

The International Shark Attack File said that in the 1950s the world averaged sixteen great white shark attacks a year. However, in the 2000s, the international average was sixty-one attacks a year. It looked like great white attacks were on the rise. But the human population was too, as were the numbers of ocean swimmers and surfers. So, in fact, per capita attack rates had actually dropped.

But, I thought, *not all the 'capita' swims, right? Not everyone has the same chance of attack; some people don't even go in the ocean.*

The statistics were confusing.

The Australian Shark Attack File said that Australia averaged about four attacks a year since records started in 1791. But in the twenty-first century, Australia averaged ten attacks per year, and in

2009 there were twenty-one attacks. So shark attacks looked like they were increasing in Australia, too. But, in the olden days, you know, they didn't have the same reporting systems that we have now, so an attack only got reported if it was significant, such as someone being hurt or killed, whereas these days they report everything. These days an 'unprovoked attack' includes a shark biting a kayak or circling a swimmer but not actually biting them. It was hard to tell what impact the change in reporting procedures and the growing human population had on shark attack statistics in Australia. Nothing conclusive stood out, except the fatality rate: the chance of death after a shark attack is 30 per cent, on average. That was consistent across both the Australian and international shark attack files.

I flicked from website to website.

Does not compute.

There was no reliable data on how many people swim or surf in the ocean, or for how long. There were no reliable estimates on shark population sizes. There was no data on the environmental factors at the time of shark attacks (salinity, water temperature, baitfish activity, clouds? No clouds? Wetsuit – black? green? grey?) No one could say what the chance of shark attack was.

Why am I bothering with this?

I took a walk, limping along the footpath. The bandages on my leg were thick and they slid over the wound with each knee bend. Something livid shot from my forearm into my non-existent hand that then cramped. Back at the house, I took oxycodone. It sat on me. I ate a block of Lisa's dad's dark chocolate with chilli, which I was not a fan of, but I finished it anyway, and I made a cup of instant coffee that tasted like sawdust, and switched the TV to something inane. I thought: *Why me?*

There have been eight recorded shark attacks at Bondi, the most of all New South Wales beaches. Two attacks were fatal. Four were prior to beach netting in 1937, and four were after that. The attacks at Bondi all occurred in the warmer months – there has never been a recorded attack in the months from May to October. All the Bondi attacks were in late afternoon or evening. I researched the weather reports on the days of those attacks; tides, swell, wind, rain, anything I could find. I graphed the data in Excel, looking for trends or hints, something that would tell me why.

I sat back. I loaded two gabapentin pills and swallowed them with Ribena. I realised why I was graphing all this spurious, spread-eagled data: I didn't want to go back in the ocean again.

Do I?

When my skin grafts were healed, and there was no longer a medical excuse, a day would come when I could go back in the ocean. *Could* go back, not *would* go back.

I pulled down the blinds and the room darkened. I took amitriptyline and Panadol. The room swam in front of me. My eyes settled on a beam of sunlight from the curtains' edge that ran diagonally to the floor and in it dust particles danced, rising and settling like distant moons in the light.

I tried to concentrate on a page of scribbled fractions that I had tortured into irrational numbers. I stared at the page until my eyes began to creep closed. My mouse drifted onto a probability website for school students and I multiplied a very small number by itself and got an even smaller number with a decimal point and fifteen zeros and then a one.

I stood. The sunbeam on the floor looked so dull and melancholy.

Are shark attacks mutually exclusive events?

Maybe the chance of two attacks on an individual was exactly the same as the chance of one attack. There was dribble on my chin. I limped to the foldout. It was 11 a.m. and it was warm in the bedroom. I lay on my back, and the foldout squeaked.

It could have happened to anyone.

Nup. It was me, wasn't it? I look like a seal.

The shark wasn't prowling around looking to attack me – it just took an opportunity on instinct, and made an error, and it got me.

Got you good, you fucken idiot. Now you've got a life of pain.

I rolled over until my left arm was underneath me. I lay on it, and it throbbed heavily, but the throbbing shut out some of the electric shocks. I gradually ascended a sleep hump into a doze, while my mouth talked to the pillow.

It's not even afternoon. It's this bad, and it's not even afternoon yet.

A weekend came and went. I saw Lisa and didn't see her. I forgot things that had been said a minute ago. I felt Lisa's baby belly rounding. I bent down to kiss it, and wondered if her belly was going to get a brown line down the middle of it, because it hadn't, and they did that, right?

On the Sunday, I writhed in six out of ten pain all night. I woke on Monday thinking, *This can't continue.*

'What's wrong?' asked Lisa

'I can't handle this pain.'

She didn't know what to say.

'It's a joke,' I said. 'Getting attacked by a shark is bad enough, but living with this pain for the rest of my life is insufferable. It's *fucked*!'

Her face crumpled into sadness, and I knew she was thinking about the future, about the baby. I thought to myself, *I can't complain like this. This can't continue.*

'How can I live with this?'

I meant it as a request for information, but when it came out it sounded like I blamed her. And, truthfully, there was a gutless part of me that wanted someone to share the fear with me, to suffer like me.

'Come on,' said Lisa, holding her nerve.

She helped me into the bathroom. I took the oxycodone. I took the gabapentin. I looked at the amitriptyline pill, and threw it away. I hated those orange ones; they flipped me out, they made me useless. I decided I'd only take them at night. I showered sitting down on a plastic chair with my eyes closed.

Lisa drove me to St Vincent's, with my arm resting on a pillow on my lap. The Plastics took the bandages off and said that the skin grafts looked good. Before we left St Vincent's, Lisa and I went up to level eight of the hospital, where a sign read: 'Navy Ward.'

The nurses in there were in uniform, and there were men in khaki carrying stiff-brimmed hats under their arms, but the patients looked the same as all the rest at St Vincent's: under white sheets, half-nude or gowned, quiet or sleeping, in discomfort, sick, sick, sick. They looked the same as I had looked, except for Paul de Gelder. He looked fit.

Paul was sitting up in his hospital bed in shorts and a t-shirt, with tattoos down his arm, and a shaved head, and his right leg was heavily bandaged. His right arm wasn't, and it looked like a clean and neat job, that amputation.

Paul's forearm had been untouched by the shark; it looked normal except that the hand was missing. Paul showed me a prosthetic arm he'd been given, at the end of which was a fake plastic hand that opened and closed a few inches. He waved it around and said, 'What do they expect me to do with this?'

And it really did look pretty useless.

Paul's main concern seemed to be navy diving. It had been suggested to him, casually, that he might like to work behind a desk for the rest of his career.

'I told them *no way*,' Paul said. 'I worked hard to be a clearance diver, and it is something I am going to do again.'

'You don't have any worries about getting back in the water?'

'None,' he replied, with a big smile. From the spark in his eye I could tell that he was genuine, and I couldn't help but laugh.

'You have a good attitude,' I said.

He shrugged. 'Well, you've got to get on with life, hey? Or otherwise be a sad sack.'

Is it maybe just not all that damn serious to lose a hand (or a leg)?

'How's your arm doing?' he asked.

I showed him my bandaged limb, swollen like a brick.

Paul held his right arm down next to his body.

'I had my hand here, by my side,' he said. 'I was swimming on my back, and it came from below and took my hand and a chunk of thigh.'

Paul had been swimming on the surface, in the open waters of the harbour, looking at the clouds. He'd crossed his arms across his chest, but thought that wasn't the safest position if he got attacked by a shark, so he put his arms by his side, and turned to check his position – and then the bull shark hit him.

'Did you see it?' I asked.

'Yeah, I saw it biting. I tried to punch it. That's when I realised my hand was gone, so then I tried to get to it with my other hand.'

'You had any nightmares?'

'Not yet,' he said, and we laughed.

Paul hadn't felt any pain when it bit him. He hadn't felt the teeth. I could relate to that. There's something in the brain that does that – the brain cuts a guy a little slack when there's a fight for life going on. Maybe there are just too many signals running up the central nervous system, and they jam up that highway so that no pain signals get through. Or maybe the adrenalin overwhelms everything. Either way, pain is not a high priority while you're being attacked by a shark.

'Are you getting much pain now?' I asked.

'Yeah.'

His pain sounded like mine: shooting electric shocks, and pins and needles. His drugs were the same, too. Paul and I had been referred to the same occupational therapist, physio and doctor, so we knew that we'd see each other around.

'He seems pretty well,' I said to Lisa when we left.

'He seems really well,' she replied.

'What a situation, you know? Another guy going through this at the same time as me.'

She nodded.

'He's got a great attitude,' I said.

That afternoon, a mobile nurse from St Vincent's visited me at home and changed my dressing.

'Sorry,' she said, 'but I have to ask. What happened to your arm?'

'I was attacked by a shark.'

Her eyes widened.

'Are you that navy diver?'

That evening, I rode the exercise bike for the first time in a while. I had stopped riding it because the drugs made me drowsy. But that night, before I took the morphine, I rode the bike for twenty minutes until I could feel sweat trickling down my back and my legs burning. The arm throbbed, but it felt good to have my heart pumping. And I thought about the question: *Why me?*

And I thought, *There is no why.*

No one could answer the question. I would never have an answer. 'Why' would drive me insane. So I decided there was no why. I had to stop thinking about it.

Lisa and I lay on the foldout bed and started a routine that had stopped with the attack. She brought out *The Book of Weeks* and turned to week twenty-three, one of the last weeks of the second trimester. The baby moved in Lisa's belly, wriggling and buzzing around, and sometimes she had hiccups too. A child was really in there. *The Book of Weeks* said the baby could hear voices from outside, so we spoke to the belly, saying, 'Hello, Buzzie Bee.'

And sometimes the baby heard, and kicked. *The Book of Weeks* showed that the baby's foot was no bigger than a pen lid, but it had grown a lot since we'd last looked at the book.

I fell asleep on my back, my arm in throbbing pain that I rated a five, but shooting occasional sevens too, but not too often. Drugs got me into a sleep that I lay through unmoving.

DAY
PLUS
33

I went back to work. This was just under five weeks after the attack, two weeks after the amputation, ten days out of hospital. I was dazed by drugs, but I just had to do something other than sit around the house. I wanted my life back. I took the bandages off my thigh in the shower. My leg was healed but still smouldered red, and I stuck on some non-stick pads with tape. I gently nudged on a pair of pants.

Lisa dropped me in the city. She was reluctant, but I'd insisted I was going to work. I walked across the courtyard of Australia Square, as a few suits milled around the fountain. Their eyes flicked from my arm to my face; maybe it was pity, or surprise, but either way it bothered me. My arm looked like a massive sausage, layers of bandages thickening it. It was a marshmallow arm, and the shadow of it was like a log.

My ego told me I was good.

You survived a shark attack, it said. *You deserve respect and praise! Goddamn shark survivor.*

I stepped into the lift feeling angry.

Everyone's looking at my arm.

I breathed in as the lift rose.

You're a victim – people will care. They love you, right?

My ego wanted reassurance, but didn't have enough confidence in itself to believe the hype. It was a bad situation for the ego.

Bloody oath, they love you! it screamed.

I breathed in. A woman in the lift met my eyes briefly, and then her eyes flicked to my arm.

You're disabled, said my inner critic.

The ego's confidence slipped down like a pair of old socks. It crumbled, disintegrated by an unspoken sentence. My arm was ruined. It was a paddle-pop stick. My heart moved faster. The lift stopped at my floor. This would be my first crowd.

Disabled. The word rushed up, and I had to swallow it.

I walked to my desk. I saw a woman and a man standing near it, talking about electricity. I felt shame rise in my face. I dropped my gaze, pretended we hadn't made eye contact, and swerved into the general manager's office.

The GM was the big boss, and a Pom, big and bright and full of charm. When he'd come to see me in the hospital, he'd kissed me on the forehead like a father would. I dropped down on a chair in his glass office and he began to prattle on with business speak that I barely heard. I watched the trading floor from the asylum of his office. I held my ruined arm from view. People milled, clicked keyboards, pointed at screens, laughed, and weren't noticing me. The GM chatted on. I felt my nerves subside a bit.

Disabled. I bounced it, that word, off myself. I felt okay.

I'm okay.

I turned to the GM.

'How are you feeling?' he asked.

'Nervous.'

'Yeah. That's why I've been prattling on like this.'

I said, 'I'm okay now.'

I walked to the trading area, and said hello to my boss and my team, and they all smiled. They didn't ask about the shark or look at my arm in a weird way. My boss had asked them not to. I had always been reserved at work, quiet (too quiet sometimes), a known introvert, and sometimes I came across as cold, I guess. I didn't often tell the people there that I liked them, that I liked being around them. I'd not been good at that, but I felt their warmth then, their genuine care, and I held back a tremor in my throat and just let myself relax.

I worked until 4 p.m. By then, a lingering tiredness had wrapped itself up into a headache, and my next round of morphine was due, as my arm got itself into an unhappy six out of ten.

DAY
PLUS
48

Lisa went back to work full-time and I missed her. We'd had so much time together and I'd got used to having her with me. Sure, it wasn't such quality time when I was all chewed up and in smoking pain, but when she went to work I missed her. It also presented a practical issue as I had appointments at St Vincent's and Randwick's Prince of Wales Hospital to get to, and getting there was a problem. The RTA had cancelled my licence when they found out that I only had one hand, even though I told them that I'd always driven one-handed. At that they were stone-faced, unamused.

'That was a little joke,' I said.

And so my mum drove an hour and a half down the freeway, then sat patiently in jerking traffic, to drive me the fifteen minutes to my hospital appointments. I told her not to worry, that I could catch a cab, but she wanted to see me. There was a part of her that felt I hadn't entirely come back from the ocean, that a part of me was still out there floundering.

Mum and I are close. She was twenty-three when I was born, which is damn young to have a kid, and she had recently moved from New Zealand to Australia, to a new place without family or friends.

My dad worked long hours, and for the first eighteen months of my life it was just her and me together, and I was her buddy. She used to say it was difficult to watch me make mistakes, because she knew she could stop them, but she believed there are some things kids need to go through alone. That attitude required a level of trust in me, and that trust turned into my independence. And I've had that feeling of independence inside me all my life. And I've taken risks, and done stupid things, and I have my regrets, but it has been a pretty rich life and all of it mine, particularly the mistakes.

After the shark attack and getting myself into shore, I'd come to feel that I had always, somewhere deep under my consciousness, believed in myself. Even though this belief had been often buried under anxiety and self-loathing, it was there when I needed it. And the seeds of it had come from those early days – just Mum and me.

Randwick's POW Hospital seems older than St Vincent's. It's a rabbit warren, full of little doors and unexpected corridors. Every intersection has four alternatives, the linoleum is faded, and it smells pungently antibacterial. There are more people wandering around, and they are either totally lost or they know exactly where they're going and are going there with a fierce determination. My first time there, I got caught in its giant sprawl for a few morphine-hazy seconds, while Mum grilled an inattentive reception lady. Then we walked along a darkening corridor, down a set of concrete stairs, and I ran into Paul de Gelder. He was resting on the landing before hopping up the next flight.

'You going to see Dr Bowring?'

I nodded.

Dr Bowring was slight, but had a strong handshake, and his manner was affable and sympathetic. I liked him from the get-go. There was a cast of people in his office: an occupational therapist, a physiotherapist, a nurse and a prosthetist (a person who makes prosthetic limbs). Mum sat in a corner, bag on her lap, and looked relaxed, like she'd been there a thousand times. I took my arm out of its sling. The nurse unwound my bandages and everyone leaned over. I expected a collective gasp when they pulled off the final layers, but it was only me who sucked in breath when the horror show came out like a half-eaten burger.

'Very good,' said Dr Bowring.

Everyone nodded, with their lips together and their bottom lips protruding.

'It doesn't look so good from here,' I said.

Dr Bowring patted me on the shoulder.

'Yes, but we're used to looking at this sort of thing.'

We started talking about the pain, because it was really bothering me. Not the pain from the surgery, but what came afterwards. After I got home from hospital. After I went back to work and started drinking again, and living. After I thought I should have been better. Dr Bowring called it 'phantom limb pain'. I could still feel my nonexistent left thumb, and all my nonexistent fingers, and the palm, even the knuckles. Often that phantom hand felt twisted with the fingers digging into each other in impossible ways, and sometimes it just curled into a tight fist and froze. Not being able to move the fingers was painful and frustrating. Sometimes I felt severe pain, like being hit by a hammer – an initial second of brilliant pain that left the hand ringing and tingling. In my worst moments, that hammer came down every few seconds and sent sharp shocks into my palm. That was unbearable.

'It's common,' said Dr Bowring. 'Well, it's common in people who have lost a limb. Phantom pain is worse if an amputation is the result of a traumatic event, and it is usually worse for upper limbs.'

I was an upper-limb amputee by shark bite, so Dr Bowring told me that I had a one in sixteen chance of living without pain, which scared me. A 6.3 per cent chance of no pain, a 93.7 per cent chance of everlasting pain – a high chance of thunderstorms and unbearable electricity in my arm for the future.

I can't live like that. It's not a life.

The vexing thing was that I *knew* the pain *was not real*. My hand couldn't hurt because it *was not there*. It was all in my head. The pain was just random, electrical signals flying about damaged nerve endings and my brain was confused by it. My brain was shocked, shocked to the shithouse, and it did not understand the signals it was being sent. It would not listen to me (and I told that stupid brain: *You're fine, we're okay, you idiot*).

Dr Bowring told me that many amputees manage phantom pain with medication for their entire lives. I looked at Mum. She was holding her breath in her chest, holding in words, and her eyes were sharp, and I looked right into them. She's a fighter, always had been.

'I want to get off the drugs,' I told him.

'That's good,' said Dr Bowring. 'That's a good attitude. But for many people drugs are the solution. Pain is a cycle, and physical pain creates a psychological response. The anxiety and fear associated with chronic pain is often what makes the pain much worse. The physical pain feeds off the psychological response and vice versa. Drugs break that cycle. But there are other methods.'

He looked at my arm and he said, 'Right now, Glenn, you need to start using your arm; you need to bump it, and touch it, and get it feeling things. It's very sensitive, and it's important that you desensitise it. And while you're doing that, it's going to hurt.'

I nodded.

He asked me what my pain score was. I said it was six, and then I said seven, then I shrugged, and I said sometimes it was nine and sometimes it was four. They all nodded as if it was no surprise at all.

The physiotherapist picked up the sling that was hanging over the back of my chair.

'You don't need this,' he said, and confiscated it.

I stood up with my elbow bent at 90 degrees, and he asked, 'Can you straighten your elbow?'

I tried, but couldn't get it past 100 degrees.

'You need to make an appointment to see me,' he said.

The physio gripped the end of my arm, and tried to force my elbow straight. A rod of pain flared and my body shuddered, and he got the elbow to about 120 degrees.

'A few appointments,' he added.

Dr Bowring and I shook hands and I said goodbye. The occupational therapist then took Mum and me down a long corridor, behind several doors and into a rectangular room that contained an extravaganza of dismembered plastic limbs sitting on filing cabinets, laying across keyboards, and sprawling all over each other on a table. The OT rummaged through the chaos, and when she opened a cupboard door a mottled artificial leg fell on her. She guffawed with laughter, and shoved it back in the cupboard. She then stretched up to a high shelf and clunked a fibreglass arm onto the table. At its end was a hook.

The hook prosthetic is a design that has survived the test of time and is a highly functional if unattractive device. The design is ingenious in its simplicity: it is opened and closed by a metal wire that runs from one side of the hook and over the shoulders. When the shoulders are rolled, the wire tightens and the hook opens. When the shoulders are relaxed the wire slackens and the hook closes because it's spring-loaded.

'I'd rather have nothing,' I said.

The OT told me that without a prosthetic I would use my right hand for everything, more than evolution had designed it for, and, over time, it might develop arthritic or carpal tunnel problems. Then I'd have no hands. I needed a prosthetic. She showed me other options: fake hands, claws, cosmetic things. Then she showed me a bionic hand – a robotic prosthesis that operates by sensing the electrical signals associated with muscle movement in the forearm. It looked lifelike, kind of, and like something I would feel okay wearing.

'That's okay,' I said.

She felt along my arm as I flexed the muscle there.

'You definitely have muscle movement,' she said.

'So I might be able to get it to work?'

She looked up. 'We'll find a way. It will take a few months to build up this muscle, though. In the meantime,' – she tapped the hook – 'don't discount this. A bionic hand will give you the look of a hand, but some amputees say that a hook is more useful. It's tougher and more durable, and if you take the time to learn how to use it, it can do some finer tasks that the bionic hand can't.'

She said that my arm was too swollen to be fitted for a prosthetic at that time, and that I'd have to wait until it reduced before it could be fitted. I was glad. I didn't want a prosthetic right away. I'd seen people wearing hooks and I'd always had to stop myself from staring. I just wasn't ready to put one on.

I left the hospital with Mum, and I asked her how I could get off the meds.

'You'll have to wean yourself off,' she said.

She wrote me a plan. I was in the most pain in the afternoon and at night, so she suggested I drop the medication in the mornings. The most important thing was to get off the morphine.

Mum drove me back home in early afternoon traffic, and by then my arm was singing in pain. Reluctantly, I took morphine and gabapentin and slept for a while. When I woke, Mum was gone and Lisa was home, sitting on the couch. It was nearly dusk. I felt groggy, but I pulled on my running shoes.

'I'm going running.'

Lisa looked up.

'You sure?'

I nodded. 'They said I could.'

I walked to the door.

'They said you could, if you stay on flat ground.'

'I will.' I opened the door.

'They said not to fall over.'

'I know, I won't.'

I could smell salt in the breeze. I pulled a tight, elastic, flesh-coloured bandage over my arm to stop it swelling, then started a slow, heavy-footed jog. A bus roared past. Blood and fluid sloshed in and out of my arm like water in a bucket. My elbow was fixed at a 90-degree angle and felt awkward. I ran to the cliffs over the sea and stared at the swell. I stopped running after thirty minutes. I was sweating and the arm was throbbing in a solid way, but it was only level-five pain and that was okay.

When I got back to the house, I sat down on the steps out the front, angry. Running for the first time was an achievement, however small, and I thought I should be happy, but it had really pissed me off. The elbow was all jammed up, and the arm was not an arm – it was some useless, broken thing, a liability. Tears of frustration came into my eyes. I blinked them away and told myself: *I am going to be as good as I was.*

Lisa watched me from just inside the door with my back to her. After a while she came out and sat with me.

That night I took out a mirror box that my OT had given me. I folded its cardboard flaps into a box, with its opening facing me, and put my left arm inside it. On the right side of the box was a mirror. In the mirror my right hand was reflected and I pretended that the reflected hand was my missing left hand. I moved the fingers of my right hand, and pretended it was my left hand that was moving in the mirror.

The mirror box was designed to trick my brain into thinking that my left hand was actually alive and moving, and that the signals coming from it were normal. I watched my fingers wriggle in the mirror, but my phantom hand, inside the box, stayed frozen. After a long session of trying to get my brain to believe that it was my phantom hand moving in the mirror, I felt one phantom finger move slightly, like some long-dead thing creeping out of a coffin and stretching in the light. For a few seconds that movement took the pain away. That blessed movement gave me hope. If I worked hard with the mirror box, I knew I could get that phantom moving. And if I could get it to move, I'd be able to get out of the pain.

The next day, I caught a taxi to see a psychologist in Paddington. A referral letter from St Vincent's asked that I be assessed for post-traumatic stress disorder.

The psychologist asked me what my fears and anxieties were. I was about to tell her about the obsession I'd had with my health, but I stopped, because I didn't have that obsession any more. I was going to tell her that I had a lot of trouble expressing my emotions, but I didn't, because I didn't have that problem any more either. So I told her I was anxious about getting back into the ocean, and about losing my right hand and having no hands. And I told her I was anxious about my ability to pick up and hold the baby. As I spoke, my sentences came out in a blather, and in the middle of a sentence that was like a projectile, the psychologist held up a hand.

'Glenn, what have you got going on? What happens day to day?'

I sat back.

I was working three or four days a week, and had appointments to see the physio twice a week and the OT twice a week, plus appointments with the Plastics. And I was studying for a one-handed driving test, and spending hours with the mirror box, as well as househunting and preparing for the baby, and loading up on sweet morphine in the afternoon.

'Plus,' I said, 'I've got these appointments with you.'

She nodded.

'That's a lot.'

'I guess.'

'Trust me, that is a lot right after a big trauma. And something has to give. Maybe that's your work? It's going to be something. Make sure it's not your recovery. Leave enough time to reflect and to come to terms with this change in your life.'

As Lisa and I lay on the foldout that night, it was muggy as hell. The fan was on but it made no difference; the humidity was intolerable. Lisa opened *The Book of Weeks*, and the baby's foot was now as big as a pen lid plus a bit. We read week twenty-five, and it was the best part of my day.

When the lights went out, and the distractions dimmed, my brain tuned in to the pain channel. I knew it was coming, and the anticipation fuelled the anxiety of it.

Don't think about it, said the rational side of my brain.

You don't own me, said the emotional side.

I wrestled myself around the bed.

'Are you okay?' asked Lisa.

I said yes, and then I took another dose of morphine and another dose of amitriptyline, and the shocks eventually came in shorter bursts.

DAY
PLUS
61

In the bowels of the Prince of Wales Hospital, I sat in an oblong-shaped waiting room that dog-legged into a smaller, trapezoidal room. Both rooms were lined with chairs and punctuated with tables of various sizes. I could not work out how those tables had got into the room. It must have been a removalist genius who transcended the torturous corridors and lift wells to get to this, the medical imaging centre.

At the end of the waiting room was a counter, behind which were a wall of files and two receptionists in blue shirts who answered constantly ringing phones. Sometimes one of the receptionists would hand a manila folder to a doctor who appeared, ghostlike, behind them in a white coat. He'd flip the folder 90 degrees, read the label and yell out a name. Someone in the waiting room would then stand and approach the counter, and all the other sick people would watch as that patient and the doctor disappeared behind a corner. Then the remaining patients would look at each other and attempt to determine if they were the next in line, or if another person in the oblong room was before them.

Lisa's phone rang and the room filled with the melody of her talking. The sick people listened. Hospital staff wheeled in a patient wearing a blue gown. He was old and tired, with a drip in his arm, and he hacked up some sputum in a terrible cough.

When the doctor came back, he called out the name of the older patient who had just been brought in. There were sighs from the sickies, who were bemused by the nonlinear nature of the queuing protocol. I was happy to wait, though, because that old guy looked so sick and uncomfortable. I gave him a lopsided smile as he was wheeled past.

Poor bugger.

I picked up my Blackberry and skimmed through emails. And Lisa, still on the phone to her mother, copied my thumb-flicking motion and raised an eyebrow, as that thumb flicking was exactly the type of movement I was supposed to limit, in case it led to RSI. I pocketed the phone.

The doctor returned and yelled out, 'Glenn Orgy-arse.'

Lisa looked at me, phone to ear, and mouthed, 'That's good!'

I had wildly jumped the queue. I stood up and walked through the room, and was shocked by the sick people looking at me. They all smiled in a lopsided fashion, and I sensed their collective mental adjunct: *You poor bugger.*

The doctor took me into an x-ray room, with giant machines of white and grey metal, and it was dark and cool in there.

'Where you from?' he asked.

'Bondi,' I said. 'Where you from?'

'China, but now Australia.'

'Good on ya.'

'What happened to your arm?'

'I got bitten by a shark.'

'Ah.' He pointed at me. 'You're the navy diver.'

After I got the x-ray, Lisa and I walked back through the labyrinth, towards the physiotherapy department. We climbed floors, went through hissing doors, and nosed our way past rushing nurses, until we found the waiting room. Lisa picked up a magazine and flicked through it in time with the minute hand on the clock above the reception desk. The clock hands revolved, tick-tocking, in quiet slowness. After a while she finished the magazine and looked at me, blowing out a sigh that flapped between her lips.

'This is fun?'

An infinitesimal, yet punishing, slice of eternity later, the physio took us into his long, narrow office. He looked at my x-ray.

'The radius and ulna are parallel,' he noted. 'Your hand is palm up.'

It took an x-ray to determine that my forearm was palm up. It was difficult to tell, just by looking, the back of my arm from the front, as skin from the back of my arm had been stretched and stitched onto the front, and vice versa, and because there was also skin from my leg now on my arm, and because of the scars.

Usually people can pronate their hands (flip them from palm up to palm down) without using their elbows, but I had lost the muscles that do that, and so my forearm was locked with one side up. I could only flip it by rolling my elbow and shoulder in an awkward shrug.

The physio gripped my arm and tried to force it to pronate, and the pain inside me groaned and flared white hot.

'You've got no real pronation,' he said. 'There may be some muscle in there. But you probably won't get much more than 30 degrees rotation.'

My freestyle stroke would always be a backstroke.

I placed my elbow on the edge of the desk, with my forearm jutting up towards the ceiling. Lisa left the room because she didn't want to see me in pain. The physio leveraged his knee up under the table and weighed down my forearm with his body weight. The scar tissue in my elbow had healed up too short, and it needed to tear so that it would regrow longer.

I was trembling with a withheld scream when he finally let me go. I reeled back in my seat and blinked away the pain.

'We got your elbow open to 130 degrees,' he said.

I was so sick of this. He stood up again.

'Let's get a few more degrees.'

The physio wouldn't humour my self-pitying moments. He wanted me to regain the full function of my elbow, because that would give me the strongest arm.

I went into the next room, and the OT gave me a trial hook prosthesis that she'd made from second-hand parts. I smiled, because it was kind of her to do it, but in my heart I knew that I could never wear that mechanical thing, not around my baby, or my wife, or in any public situation. I couldn't see that its usefulness would ever overcome my fear of what it said about me: that I was disabled.

·

DAY
PLUS
64

Vic Peddemors, the marine biologist from the Department of Primary Industries, came to visit. He arrived at Lisa's parents' place with a big cardboard box and sat it on the dining room table.

'I brought these along to explain why I concluded that it was a great white that attacked you.' Vic pulled shark jaws out of the box.

Lisa said, 'Okay, I'm going now.' She went into the kitchen and I stared at the jaws.

Decent chops.

Vic put three sets of jaws on the table, all of them from 2.5-metre sharks. The first set was from a bull shark; it was a wide jaw, roughly in the shape of a love heart, and its teeth were pointy and serrated. The next set was from a tiger, and was oval-shaped, longer in height than in width, and the teeth were the same size as the bull shark's but were curved like a hook. The last set was from a great white, also oval-shaped, like the tiger shark's. They measured about 50 centimetres by 30 centimetres – big enough to slip over my head – and it was the teeth that stood out, the size of them. They were bigger than the other sharks', particularly the bottom teeth, which were the size of large, flat corn chips.

'Each shark has teeth evolved for different types of prey,' said Vic. 'The great white has big, triangular, pointy teeth that crisscross like steak knives. A 2.5-metre white is beginning to eat marine mammals and its teeth are designed to bite into large chunks of fat and flesh.'

Lisa, who was in the other room, and supposedly not listening, heard this.

'So does that mean that Glenn was lucky to get away?' she asked.

'Yeah. Very lucky.'

She frowned.

There was something Vic had said to me while I was in the ICU that had stuck in my head – that I was lucky it was a great white, because they rarely take a second bite.

Those words had comforted me then, because they meant that it had just been a test bite, it was shark error, and nothing personal. I reminded Vic of his words, and he said, 'Very occasionally a shark will bite multiple times. And in those cases, it's clearly not mistaken identity. But generally, humans are not on their menu. I think about 95 per cent of shark attacks are due to mistaken identity.'

'I thought they had good eyesight, though?'

'They do. They see much better than us underwater, but think about what they see. Remember, they're usually deep, maybe 5 metres down, and with the light coming from above they only see a silhouette. They see something big and slow, and the juvenile great white is just learning to attack mammals, so it's not an expert.'

'Then it did a good job to get my arm so accurately.'

'It wasn't going for your arm,' he said. 'It was going for the whole of you. That it got your arm was lucky – otherwise it would have been your body. The shark came from behind you, and as your arm was extending through the water, it bit through your wrist with one corner of its mouth, the rest of its jaw clamped on your forearm, and the other corner of its mouth missed your arm altogether.'

Using his hands, he showed me what he meant.

I took this in. 'In hospital, I'd been thinking that it was something about me. You know, my shape, or scent, or something – that was why it went for me . . .'

'Nah,' he said. 'It wasn't because you're special. It wasn't because you married a girl from the eastern suburbs, and have been eating at the fancy cafes in Bondi, or anything like that. It was just wrong place, wrong time. We're not sure exactly why they attack, Glenn. There is still so much we don't know about sharks. For instance, there has never been a pregnant great white examined by a scientist.' He shrugged. 'We know so little.'

I asked Vic about the 'dusk and dawn' warnings for avoiding sharks. 'Do you think surfers listen to them?'

'No,' he said, 'but we have to warn people that dusk and dawn are dangerous. Light plays a role in the food chain. Bulls and tigers in particular feed in changing light. Great whites feed during the day. But, still, dawn and dusk are the times when the most feeding is happening.'

'Those are the best times of day to surf,' I said.

'I know. My mates and I go surfing at 6.30 in the morning.'

'So you surf at dawn?'

'Well, I wait until the sun is above the horizon.'

'I used to try to get in first, in the dark still, before anyone else.'

'Not me,' he said, shaking his head. 'I can't do that; I think I know too much.'

Vic left then, with his cardboard box of jaws.

I wait until the sun is above the horizon. I took comfort from those words, thinking that if it was good enough for a shark expert, it was good enough for me. Maybe I could get back in the water after all.

I received an email from James McIntosh. I'd read about James in newspaper articles, and from his quotes I could tell he was the guy who had helped me out of the water. He'd sent through his phone number and I gave him a call. It was a phone number from up on the north coast of New South Wales, and he answered with sounds of a party in the background. I yelled down the receiver until he heard me, and his voice became clearer as he stepped away from the noise.

'Oh, yeah,' he said. 'Oh, right, how are you?'

The night of the attack came back to me through his voice: the backwash, falling to my knees in the shore break. His voice was ingrained. We talked and he told me his story and parts of my story.

'Have you been back in the water?' I asked.

'Yeah, but it wasn't for a while. I had a break, you know.'

'Did you think I was going to die?'

'I don't know, man. You did – you thought so. I didn't really con-sider it until you told me to tell your wife you loved her. Then I just didn't know. I'd never seen anything like that before.'

'Yeah.'

'After the ambulance left, everyone just stood around, and the newspapers were there asking questions. People were shaking hands, and someone hugged me, but I just needed to get out of there. I walked to the showers and washed the blood off, and then went home and turned everything over in my head. It was terrible. I've been thinking about contacting you, but I didn't want to . . . You know.'

'Yeah.'

I got the sense he had more to say, and we agreed we'd meet up when he was next in Bondi.

I hung up the phone, and it was dark. The balcony door was open. I stood outside with the sounds of crickets in the grass and aeroplanes in the sky.

James had reacted on instinct when he came to help me. He didn't think about the blood or gore. At times the value of life can seem so little; news stories of human suffering give me a sense that sometimes humanity is malignant. But James proved otherwise, and

so did the other people on the beach that night. They saved a life –
strangers saving a stranger. It took guts. The horror was awful.

Those who came to help were mostly uninitiated and untrained;
they jumped in the deep end, maybe in an extreme way that will
only come once in a lifetime. When the ambulance drove away, and
they were left behind, and the adrenalin wore off, and they washed
off the blood, I'm sure it wasn't over. They had the images to deal
with and the questions that have no answer: *Did I do the right thing?*
Could I have done more? The bone and blood, the shaking pale surfer
– the one similar to them. At the moment of their commitment to
save my life, they also unwittingly committed to ongoing replays of
the shark attack that might never go away. Behind their actions were
courage and compassion, two of the greatest human virtues.

I closed the balcony door.

Lisa was on the foldout bed, resting on her side. I lay down and
put my hand on her belly.

'How was he?' she asked.

I nodded. 'Good. But it must have been tough for the people
there that night.'

'They were amazing.'

'Fucken.'

She frowned, pointing at her belly. 'Don't swear.'

It was warm in the room, and the fan was nice, and traffic bumbled past outside. Lisa read from *The Book of Weeks*: week
twenty-seven. The baby's foot was still small enough that I could circle it with my finger and thumb. I loved that child in there, who was
already real to me. I shut my eyes.

Find a house, make an offer, negotiate, inspect, exchange a contract,
get a loan, move. Buy a pram, cot, bassinette, baby clothes, change table,
bouncer . . .

I felt needles start in my hand, and tried to resist the pain coming. But it came, as it always did.

DAY
PLUS
79

I saw the psychologist again and she wanted to talk about self-image, and I thought, *Here comes a can of worms.*

The psychologist asked me if losing my hand had damaged my self-image. I had certainly had moments when I felt all eyes were on me, when I felt different, stared at, pitied. I admitted to that. But I told her those feelings had not lasted that long. I'd already stopped noticing people looking at me. And that had happened because I was, kind of, proud of myself, proud that I had survived, and I had that to hang on to.

A chain of people contributed to saving my life, but it had started with me. I'd paddled in. In the ocean I'd been as terrified as I could be, and in hopeless moments I'd waited for the world to turn black. But I'd gotten away and back to the beach, and I got my life back by doing that, and it didn't matter that I'd lost a hand to do it. I'd survived. That's why I walked around unashamed. I felt like I'd done something good.

I told the psychologist I wanted to surf again. I knew I could force myself into the water, but I was worried that I wouldn't enjoy it. She told me to go down to the edge of the ocean and see how

I felt, and to let whatever I did feel sit inside me without resisting it – just to let it pass, if I could.

When I got my driver's licence back, I drove Lisa to the Central Coast to visit my parents. I had my arm resting on a pillow on my lap, and the first hour was peaceful. It was the middle of the day, and my morphine gauge was on zero. I had only a few gabapentin holding down the fort. The pain had been fours out of ten for most of the drive, not too heinous, but then I felt shards of six pain start up that wouldn't dim. I lifted my arm and straightened it to its new 174-degree limit.

'You okay, honey?'

'Yep.'

Then at a traffic light a nine pain hit. My arm involuntarily jumped up off the pillow into the air and drew itself in tightly to my chest. Lightning exploded. I clutched my arm across my stomach and concentrated on driving.

'Are you okay?'

I took my foot off the pedal and the car slowed to 40. I pulled over near a roundabout.

'Glenn, what's the matter?'

I shook my arm until it throbbed.

'I'm okay,' I said.

'Do you want me to drive?'

'We're almost there.'

I drove on and every few minutes my phantom hand twisted itself into an uncomfortable position, the thumbnail digging into the palm, the fingers crossing and locking together in an impossible fist.

When we arrived at my folks' place, I took some low-dose morphine that I knew would be no defence against nine pain. It took hours of shocks before the hand settled down from the drive. Lisa and Mum fussed around me. Eventually I had a morphine dream on the couch and woke in the late afternoon, feeling lethargic, with tendrils of melancholy holding on to me. I made myself go for a walk.

I walked down a tar hill in bare feet, board shorts and a t-shirt that was flapping in the wind. It was dusk by the time I reached the sand. Low, voluminous clouds moved slowly in the sky and behind them was a high void filled with white light that might have gone on forever. It was cool and salt spray came off the waves and drifted in the wind. Sand squeaked as my feet twisted in and gripped the granules. The surf was clean despite the wind and it was big and breaking on deep banks into lines of rolling white water. I jogged towards the north of the beach, to where the rocks started and the beach and clouds and the forested headland disappeared into a tiny corner. I ran high up on the sand away from the water and I felt no fear. I felt nothing except blood filling my arm with a solid throb.

The sand thinned as I approached the northern corner and it began to tilt towards the sea, with the waves lapping over it, drenching the sand, turning it grey, and washing away my footprints. A wave broke and raced up over my feet and I felt nothing when that salt water touched me, only its cool tingle and its itch.

At the rock shelf, the sand took a right turn, and in that little corner at the end of nearly everything were two surfers, 20 metres out, surfing on a punchy re-form. The sea around them was wild. Out the back, white water jumped into the air and landed over rocks, with some of it running in lines towards the beach. Smaller waves fattened up and re-formed. Bigger waves barged their way over the deeper section and came at the surfers in full flight, and they had to duck under those bigger ones, disappearing into dark water.

I edged towards the sea, watching the surfers. The waves they caught were short and quick, and they turned and banged and shot spray up into the air. The sea ran up over my shins as I watched them surf. My feet sank into the sand. I didn't think about my arm. I watched the surfers crawling on the dark ocean, fighting the rip to stay in position. I thought about the ocean below them, and their nonchalance, and I thought that I felt okay standing knee-deep, but I wasn't sure about out there. A sliver of anxiety reached into my heart.

Lucky it wasn't a bigger shark.

I stood still. Nothing else like that thought came again, and I left the beach wanting to be in the water again.

A few days later, I drove to the pool with Lisa. My skin grafts were healed, or healed enough for swimming; I was watertight. I changed in the locker room while Lisa waited by the pool. There were others in the change room, from some kind of water polo training. I stripped the bandages off my arm and could feel them staring, but I stood up straight. I walked out to the pool, in the echoing hall.

There was a moment as I first sank into the shallow end of the pool when I felt a shiver up my back. I immersed myself underwater, and saw there were only the legs of swimmers kicking, no sharks at all.

I swam for twenty minutes. My left arm sliced through the water without carrying much, but it felt good to roll that shoulder over and get the blood to pump through it. I thought I might swim in a crooked line, but I didn't. I thought it might hurt when I slapped the skin grafts on the water, and there was some discomfort, but it went away.

When I got out of the pool I almost fell. My whole body was exhausted. I stumbled over to Lisa and she wrapped a towel around my shoulders.

'Great swimming!'

She took photos as I sat, spent, on the bench, in my speedos.

'Come on, honey,' I said. 'This is not my best look.'

After we got home, I stood on the balcony and watched the sun set over the harbour.

I'm back swimming. I'm back on track.

For a while it rained lightly through scattered cloud, then the sky went pink, and then the clouds closed over and the rain got heavy. It made me feel calm watching the raindrops on the water. It reminded me of times when I had sat on my surfboard at dusk, bobbing gently out the back, oblivious to anything below, the sky darkening, the water turning into glass; I had never been more at peace. I could recall that feeling – it was still alive for me. I knew I might not ever surf alone again, and maybe never without fear, but I wanted to surf at dusk again, and watch the clouds fold into black, and catch a glass wave to shore, and run up the cold sand.

Despite what had happened, and what might yet happen, dusk is the time of day when I feel most alive.

DAY
PLUS
86

Lisa's cousin, a physiotherapist, sent me a transcutaneous electrical nerve stimulation machine, with a note that said that it was for pain relief. The idea was to connect a suite of electrodes to the back of my neck and blast the nerves there with enough electrical noise to jam up the pain gate and stop nerve messages being sent from my phantom hand to my brain. Essentially it was designed to replace the pain signals with a more bearable form of electrical stimulation from the machine. The machine had frequency and intensity dials and switches, and it could pulse or burst or flow. I put the sticky pads on the back of my neck, set the intensity to medium, left the frequency on the standard setting, and pressed 'flow'. A gentle buzzing started on my neck, my muscles twitched and danced, and instantly the pain went entirely out of my arm.

Zero.

I closed my eyes and indulged in the nothingness. And that lasted for fifteen full seconds. Then the pain returned: three, four, five, and it sat at five. I turned up the dials of the machine. I switched it from pulse to blast. But the pain didn't go away again. It stayed at five.

I told my OT about the machine, and she led me through the

hospital until we arrived at the transcutaneous electrical nerve stimulation clinic, which had fields of beds with people in them, all taped up to machines and learning to use them. A nurse, a machine expert, strapped me to the latest model and tried out different locations for the sticky pads and all the frequencies, but it didn't make any difference. The pain sat at five. And despite the initial fifteen-second success with the machine at home, it never worked that well again, even when I turned it up to a level that was unbearable, the sticky pads getting hot, my shoulders muscles trembling. So I gave up on it giving me zeroes, but I could keep the pain at a five and that was good. It was good to know I could use the machine when I was in real pain. That gave me the confidence to drop my dosage of morphine in the mornings, and to drop amitriptyline altogether.

Lisa and I went on a prenatal course in the Blue Mountains. There was a selection of plush chairs set in a circle around a carpeted room, and tinkling, calming music playing. The midwife running it had over twenty years of experience 'birthing cherubs', as he put it.

The pregnant women sat in low leather reclining chairs, with their partners next to them on more upright chairs. Lisa and I got there last and so we both ended up in leather recliners. Everyone was asked to introduce themselves, with the midwife first checking their names and then posing other random questions. The partners answered while holding their wives' hands or rubbing their bellies. When it came to me, the midwife asked me who I was and what I was there for. I pushed up out of my chair and tried to touch Lisa's belly, but she was sunk deep into her chair 2 feet away and my shortened arm had no chance. I slunk back into my chair. I'd taken some morphine after the drive.

'I'm Glenn,' I said. My head felt like a lollipop on my neck. 'I'm here to learn about birth.'

The course ran all morning. I didn't realise what a convoluted path it was through the birth canal. I mean, I knew it was a difficult tunnel, but I didn't know there were twists and turns, and posterior and anterior presentations, and a little monitor they put on the belly to keep track of the baby's heartbeat. During a coffee break, Lisa and I had a word with the midwife, who was an approachable guy. Lisa told him about the situation with the shark. She told him about the scans she'd had in hospital.

'Do you think my stress levels could have hurt the baby?' she asked him.

The midwife said that babies were tougher than we give them credit for. He said that the baby may have experienced a brief period of stress, but would be fine. He had seen examples of dire situations, including the traumatic amputation of a pregnant woman's arm, and the baby had come out a few months later all okay. I don't know if his words helped Lisa that much, because she really just needed to see the baby, in her arms, but I think he gave her some momentary relief from the worry.

The midwife looked at my arm.

'Do you get phantom pain, Glenn?'

'Fucken,' I said.

Lisa nudged me, but the midwife smiled. And then he started talking about neuroplasticity, which is the brain's ability to adapt to change – to be malleable. I'd never heard of it, but from what the midwife said it sounded like it might help my phantom pain.

The neural wiring of the brain happens during gestation, when the brain and the body are connected up by some intensely complicated system of synaptic pathways. And it had long been believed that once the synaptic pathways were wired they were unchangeable. So, if they were disturbed or broken, a person might be left without function, without sight, or balance, or speech, or they could lose the ability to interpret the signals from a lost hand. However, scientists had begun to talk of new therapies that could rewire synaptic pathways, and teach blind people to see, deaf people to hear and stroke victims to talk. The scientists studying neuroplasticity were coming up with ways to teach the brain to relearn and reinvent itself.

I'm no brain scientist, but in simple terms the brain has three parts. Firstly, the lizard brain, that remnant of human evolution, the pre-verbal brain stem sitting on top of the spinal cord; the lizard brain has been honed by eons of evolution and is programmed with a human history of instinct and reflex, and is unthinking, unemotional, and functions purely to maintain our life support. On top of the lizard brain is the limbic system, which manages our basic emotional responses to stimuli (fear, anger, response to pain). And on top of that is the bulky part of our brain, the neocortex, which is the seat of reason and thought, and of our higher intelligence. And these three parts are synaptically wired together, and also to some other parts as well, and they all rely on each other. One mechanism of connecting the bits that has been researched extensively is cortical maps, or brain maps. These are the ways the brain determines where in the body a piece of sensory input is coming from.

When the sensory input from my left hand was unplugged from the mainframe, by the shark, the brain map for my hand went berserk. Confusion ensued. The lizard brain, reflexively, tried to sort it out.

'Clench,' said the lizard. But the hand did not send a signal back.

'Are you in pain?' the lizard asked it.

No answer.

'*Are you in pain?*'

No answer.

'Hey. You're in pain, aren't you?'

No answer.

'*YOU'RE IN PAIN!*'

The lizard fired off various pain shocks, which I felt in my non-existent hand, but which were actually coming from my lizard brain. The limbic system received these pain messages, and went on to decide that I was very sad, angry and fearful about this. The neocortex tried to calm this escalating process down, but by then it was too late and the lizard brain and my limbic system had started a raging bushfire of pain panic that only soothing milligrams of morphine could hose down.

After my hand had been amputated, its brain map began to dwindle away. And that freed up some of my brain's processing capacity, and other brain maps began to take over my hand map's previous territory. A neuroscientist, V.S. Ramachandran, had found that the brain map for the face can invade the space left by an amputated hand's map. He had examined a boy who'd lost his hand in a car crash, and what bothered this boy most about the amputation was an itch in his phantom palm that he couldn't scratch. Ramachandran, testing the face map's ability to invade the hand map's previous territory, scratched the boy's face with a pen. The boy felt the scratching in his phantom palm and was able to get relief from the itch.

I went and found a pen. I scratched it all over my face. Oh, I scratched like a madman. The pen left red marks on my face, but I didn't get any sensation in my phantom hand, and it stayed clenched.

Come on, face map. Invade. Invade.

Ramachandran has also discovered a potential solution to the problem of frozen phantom limbs: mirror box therapy. I read that and thought, *Not working for me . . .*

I'd worked with the mirror box every day and it hadn't helped that much with the pain. I'd only been able to slightly move my frozen fingers. But after reading that the brain can take a very long time to retrain, I decided to continue with mirror box therapy for as long as it took to get the phantom hand moving.

Several days later, with thoughts of neuroplasticity still in my mind, I took a long shower. I rarely took long showers, but the weather was cooling and I'd got into the habit of standing under the running water. It calmed me. I stood with my head tilted to the right and the spray hit me square against my left shoulder and chest. I wasn't aware I'd started doing that, as I usually let the water hit me on top of my head, crawl over my tilted face, and launch onto the tiles.

I dried off in the narrow bathroom, and an answer to a question that I hadn't even asked myself popped into my neocortex:

I could feel that warm water flowing over my left hand.

I stood still for a moment, realising that I had felt warmth in my phantom hand – not a strong sensation, but it was there. I could feel the hot water on my chest in my hand. I wrapped a towel around my waist and went into the kitchen, opened the freezer, put some ice in a bag and rubbed it over my chest. A flood of coolness flowed into my hand. My frozen fist opened. My head lolled back and I took a deep breath. I sat down against the cupboard as the pain drained away to just a tingle, just a two.

All night I held the ice against my chest, finding the most sensitive places. I stuck it up under my arm, and lay down with it in bed. No morphine, no amitriptyline, just a few gabapentin, and I slept in glorious two pain.

DAY
PLUS
108

Luke and I met up on the Central Coast. He parked in my parents' driveway and we stood leaning on the bonnet of his four-wheel drive.

'How'd you get in?' he asked.

'Paddled.'

He shook his head.

'Only you would do that, mate.'

We laughed. 'Well, there wasn't much choice, really,' I added.

And then I asked him, outright, 'What went wrong, way back, that stopped us talking for a decade?'

He had a vigorous answer and I made myself listen, and some of it I found hard to listen to, because he seemed angry and I thought I was the one with that right. But some of what he said was correct. Some of it was my fault. I had a worse streak of stubbornness than he did. I felt sad then, and only said that it was a hell of a friendship to have had fall apart.

Then we just said nothing, and stood against the car. There was no easy end to the complex dynamic that had stalled our friendship for so long, but we agreed that we'd said what we wanted to say, and that was it; the end of the elephant in the room. We were different, our lives were different, but we'd had a crack at really clearing the air. I think we knew there was some friendship left to be salvaged. I gave him a hug. You know, we'd grown up like brothers; I loved the guy.

We went to the Terrigal pub and met up with some school mates I hadn't seen for a while. I relaxed and listened to where they were up to in their lives, and we had some laughs. Before I left, Luke asked me, 'Will you surf again?'

'Dunno,' I said. 'I'll try. I don't know if I will enjoy it.'

'I saw your mate, that navy diver, surfing,' said Luke.

'Where?'

'It was in the paper. Last Wednesday.'

Back at my parents' house I found Wednesday's paper, and there was a picture of Paul de Gelder hopping out of the ocean at Bondi with a surfboard. He looked happy. I read the article a few times, and something moved around in my chest, some kind of pent-up feeling. I sent Paul a text message and he said he'd loved the experience.

The next day Lisa and I went to the Point. I didn't have board shorts with me because I hadn't planned on swimming, so I wore pyjama shorts. We walked down the hill to the sand and sat on the beach near the Point. It was a clear day, blue sky, and there were two coal tankers on the horizon. I took my wedding ring off my right hand and gave it to Lisa. The waves were small. It was high tide and there was deep water close to the edge. The water washing onto the shore was white and brown where the sand coloured it, and then out a little further the sea was green, and deeper still it was an azure blue that ran off to the horizon.

I stood on the wet sand, which was hard and crisscrossed with the rivulets that formed when the shore sucked back into the sea. I stood for a while, and then I just ran. I ran towards a looming unbroken wave as it stood up in the green, and it was beautiful, with the sun almost shining through it to the sand below. I dove into its belly.

I swam out to where the water was deep and I couldn't stand. I trod water and watched the horizon and the small waves rolling over the Point. I lay on my back and floated, my feet towards the sky, the sun on my face. I closed my eyes and floated in the green, not far from shore, just gliding there, my ears below the water, with the sound of nothing.

For Lisa's birthday on 27 May we went to a flash pizza restaurant. We relived old times: we'd had one of our first dates in that same restaurant, back when we hardly knew each other, two months before we got engaged. Lisa made jokes about the frozen bravado I'd had then. In the darkness, at our outdoor table, near the road and the passersby, and in the coolness of that May evening, everything swarmed around us unnoticed while we picked apart that old personality of mine. This caused a great deal of hilarity, mostly for Lisa, but it was her birthday, so whatever.

Lisa stretched, her arms reaching high, and groaned.

'My back,' she complained.

Pregnancy had caused her back problems to flare up again. She and I both suffer recurring lower back problems that tend to go away and come back again like dormant wisdom teeth.

'You should go and see Louise,' I suggested.

She nodded. 'You know, maybe you should see her, too – she might be able to help with your arm. You can't walk around rubbing an icepack on your chest for the rest of your life.'

Lisa had discovered Louise, a physiotherapist, in 2007, when Louise achieved results quickly with Lisa's bad back. I had just moved in with Lisa at that stage, and my back had also packed it in and wouldn't get any better, so I'd gone to see Louise. She didn't ask me what was wrong, but it might have been obvious from the way I hobbled into her office that day. She made me take my shoes off, and asked me to turn around with my back to her.

'Shake your body,' she said.

I gave my arse a little wriggle and rolled my shoulders.

'No, like this,' she said. I looked over at Louise as she flailed about. I took a breath, and wriggled my body and jiggled my head.

'No, shake your body like you've just been shocked by electricity, or you're being reborn.'

I froze. I heard the clock tick.

I upped my performance a full fifth and gave my entire body a loosening shake, and even lifted one leg off the ground. And then I stood still. Louise walked around the front of me, tipped my chin into the air, then walked to the back again.

'When did you hurt your ankle?'

I looked at my ankles, which were covered by my pants.

'Years ago,' I said. 'I damaged the ligaments. I couldn't walk on it for weeks.'

'Have you had an operation on that knee?' she asked, touching my left knee.

I froze. *How'd she know that just by looking at me?*

'Arthroscopy,' I said. 'I had chipped bone removed.'

She put her hands on my shoulders.

'You were traumatised when you broke your nose, weren't you?'

She was staring at me, right in the eyes, and she looked sad. I said, 'I guess so.'

I lay on a table, with Louise touching my ankles. I couldn't follow what she was doing. She touched one ankle, pressed it gently, gave it a tiny massage, and then she did the same to the other ankle, and then the same to my knees. I was about to explain that it was actually my lower back that was killing me, but she snapped on a rubber glove and asked me to open my mouth. She put her thumbs into my mouth and pressed painfully into its roof. I gripped the side of the table.

'Wha arr ooh ooing?' I asked.

'I'm stretching the muscles of your soft palate.'

'Wharr?'

She massaged my inner mouth, and my face, for fifteen minutes. Then she told me that I was to walk around pretending I had a billiard ball in my mouth, and I was to project my nose when I walked.

'Walk around like you're trying to make your nose grow.'

When I went to see her again, a few days later, she said, 'How's the back?'

'Fantastic,' I replied. 'Much, much better.'

Normally my back took as long as six weeks to mend, but three days of walking round like Pinocchio had fixed it.

'Well,' she said, 'your posture was all wrong. Your ankles and knees were out of alignment, but it was mostly that broken nose of yours. Breaking your nose is very traumatic, because it's such a sensitive feature in the middle of our image of ourselves. And when you broke your nose, you changed your posture. You began to walk with your head tilted down. You were trying to protect your nose. After years of doing that, it has affected your back – the back is the place where our trauma and anxieties go.'

Louise hadn't needed to see me again; she had fixed my back.

At the pizza restaurant, on Lisa's birthday, as we finished dinner, my pain started to rear up, so we left. I apologised to Lisa, because it was her last birthday before becoming a mother. It should have been a special night. My pain just always seemed to intervene. I decided that I would go see Louise again. It was a long shot; I'd already seen a team of doctors who'd said that phantom pain was just the way it was. But I wanted to try something different.

Louise had heard about the shark attack, and she thought she could help me with the pain. I unwrapped my bandages and she asked me to close my eyes, while she pressed on the muscle of my arm and ran her hands over my shoulder and chest.

'Does your hand feel like it's locked into a fist?'

'Yes,' I said.

'Like this?' She held up a fist with the tip of the thumb poking between the knuckles of the index and ring fingers.

'Exactly.'

'I can feel tension there.' She pressed down hard. 'The thumb is the worst, isn't it?'

'Yep.'

'What else?'

I told Louise about the drugs. I'd already stopped taking morphine and amitriptyline, but I was still on gabapentin. I wanted off that too.

'I want you to get off that,' she agreed.

We discussed a plan to lower my dosage. Louise thought that working with the mirror box would eventually succeed, but she wanted me to change the way I used it.

'Make only tiny movements in the mirror,' she said. 'Make only the movements that you feel your left hand can do, even if it's just a tiny wiggle.'

Over the next few weeks, Louise had me concentrate on the muscles in my right hand. With my right hand, she made me bring the tips of my fingers and thumb together.

'Now close your eyes and pulse them,' said Louise, 'squeeze and release.'

I pulsed.

'Make a little noise while you're doing it. Go "Hmm, hmm, hmm" while you're pulsing.'

I closed my eyes. 'Hmm, hmm, hmm.'

'Try to feel exactly what every muscle in your right arm is doing. Not just in your hand, but in your forearm and shoulder as well.

Concentrate on the movement in the fingers, in the wrist. Concentrate on how the parts come together.'

'Hmm, hmm, hmm.'

'That's it.'

Louise had her fingers pressed into my forearm.

'Keep going,' she told me. 'Make your left arm watch your right arm.'

I told my lizard brain to focus.

'Now make your left hand do the same thing your right hand is doing. Touch the fingers to the thumb.'

And, slowly, the phantom fingers of my left hand curled towards my phantom thumb, and the thumb swung from left to right to meet them. I couldn't quite get them to touch.

'That's it,' Louise encouraged. 'Now pulse your left hand in time with your right.'

I pulsed my hands. I could feel my left hand stirring slightly, and it sent a zing of energy and muscle movement up my forearm. It was a physical joy, and a joy in my heart, to be freely moving that phantom hand. I was in control of a ghost. The lizard was getting feedback from the fingers; the lizard was happy. I pulsed that left hand harder and harder. I opened and clenched a fist. I forgot about pulsing my right hand.

'No,' said Louise.

And then my left hand slowed, and then it froze.

'No, no,' she repeated. 'You have to pulse both hands at the same time, and gently. Your right hand is showing your left how to do it.'

After we finished each of those sessions, I wandered out onto the street in a daze. Moving the fist was one of the most satisfying experiences I'd ever had. It left me wiped out, like a long run, or a three-hour exam. Straight after the sessions my fist would freeze again, but I was okay with that, because I knew it could move. When I got home from work each night, I used the mirror box and could get the hand moving, slowly and painfully. But after twenty minutes the pain died down. I'd finish up in two pain and take only a few gabapentin before bed.

Lisa and I moved into a new house, in Bondi. We had been living at her parents' place for six months, and they had been fantastic, the best parents-in-law a bloke could want. But it was exciting to be moving into a place of our own. Actually moving house, though, was a bitch. Oh, everyone knows that. Gas, electricity, cleaning, packing, unpacking, cardboard boxes, tape (*Why did I use so much tape?*), the smell of fresh Pine O Cleen on the floor, realising upon opening the fridge that it hadn't been entirely clean while it had been sitting in storage, lugging shit upstairs only to be told, 'Honey! All that stuff is staying down here.'

'Nah, better up here, I reckon.'

'*No!*'

The swelling in my arm had reduced, my forearm had become stable, so I'd been fitted for a prosthesis and had finally received a hook. It looked strange, I have to say, but I wore it anyway. The removalists tried not to look at it as we scuttled past each other in the hallway. The hook was helpful for lifting and opening boxes, and cutting off packing tape. It was also strangely comfortable. I got this kind of a confidence from working with it, as it was the first time I had operated with two arms in months. It was a cool day but I got sweaty, and it felt good.

The removalists brought in the last box – a brand new 60-inch LCD television.

'Where to, boss?'

'Just here,' I said.

They put it in the living room, before a big white wall.

'We're all done, boss.'

'Thanks, fellas.'

They left, and Lisa, bringing in various tchotchkes from the car, ran into them on their way.

'Your husband is doing well, with that hook and all,' they told her.

Meanwhile, I stood in front of the big white wall, surrounded by a sea of brown boxes and bubble wrap. I tightened the band on my hook and kicked open my toolbox. *Seinfeld* was on in an hour.

Goddamn, I am going to hang this TV on the wall.

I ripped my steel hook along the TV's cardboard box and tore it open. Streams of packing foam burst out at me. That TV weighed 20 kilos. I lifted it out of the box and it slipped around precariously on my hook, and I worried that I didn't have a good grip on it. But I gripped it viciously and crabbed across the lounge-room floor with it in my arms until I was in the corner. I then stood on the second step of a ladder and drilled into the white wall, red dust spinning out of the wall onto my face and chest and sticking in my sweat. Lisa came and watched while the drill screamed and spun between the grip of my tongs. I drilled six holes in the wall, and then I affixed the bracket. There were five minutes left until *Seinfeld* was on. Now I had to lift the TV onto the bracket on the wall. I considered lifting it by myself, but I needed to get it to shoulder height. It was too big, and awkwardly shaped, and I knew the hook wasn't capable of that. So I called over to my seven and a half months pregnant wife.

'*Honey!*'

Lisa was polishing a fifty-year-old family heirloom that was going to be placed, with several other forty-year-old family heirlooms, in an inconvenient place.

'Yes?' she asked.

'Can you give me a hand with this?'

We lifted the television onto the bracket. The look on Lisa's face would have been priceless if we both hadn't been terrified about dropping that expensive TV onto the floorboards. With some jiggling, and husband-wife-type shorthand facial communication, we got it to lock onto the bracket, and the bastard was hung. We drifted back to the kitchen to admire the black oblong against the white wall. Red dust covered the floor and the windows, and my beard.

Magnificent. What a hook!

'It looks a bit wonky,' said Lisa.

'That's just a trick of the light.'

'It looks like that end is lower than the other end?'

I got out my tape measure. The bottom-left corner was 2 centimetres lower than the right corner.

We took the TV off the wall. The bracket was half a centimetre off level.

'Ah, shit,' I said.

Lisa kissed my gritted cheek.

'Keep it up,' she said.

I drilled another six holes in the wall, making twelve holes total. That wall was one punctured son of a bitch. Still, I'd got the TV level. I missed *Seinfeld*, but, damn, I felt good that I'd hung that telly.

That moving day was tiring. The place was a shambles when we finished up. Boxes that had been marked 'Plates' were half filled with plates and half with books. There were no flyscreens, no bathroom mirrors, no phone, no internet. I'd worn my boots on the white carpet and left red footprints at the bottom of the stairs. But it was okay, because we were in. We'd get it all set up before the baby came. I felt a great sense of contentment. I knew that Lisa and I would turn this shell into a home.

I set up our bed and we folded into it. I dropped my dusty hook on the bathroom floor. My left arm and shoulder ached in a good way, in a useful way, after a full day of work. It was quiet and cool, and Lisa opened up *The Book of Weeks* at week thirty-four. I rubbed her belly and could feel the baby moving to the sound of her voice. I fell asleep listening to her read.

DAY
PLUS
116

Winter came. Offshore winds blew all day. I'd got myself down to four gabapentin pills a day and, with Louise's help, I'd learnt to wriggle my phantom fingers. That was freedom; when pain came, I wriggled the fingers and it lessened. Sometimes I even forgot about the pain, but the instant I became aware that I'd forgotten, it would return. I usually only felt a baseline of pins and needles that registered as a three. Moving my fingers didn't get rid of that, but three pain was okay. It was just those damn gabapentin tablets. I couldn't stop them. Without them the pain turned into sharp electrical shocks. I was improving, though; I could feel it. I was pushing my pain barrier, testing it. I wasn't as afraid.

I asked Damo if he wanted to go for a surf.

'I've been waiting for you to ask that,' he said. 'You ready?'

'I have no idea,' I replied.

I had practised 'popping' up off the ground into a surfing stance, but I felt unbalanced even on stable ground and had no idea how I'd go in the ocean. Mostly, though, I was worried that I'd freak out.

The night before I went surfing, Lisa and I went into a local surf shop to buy a wetsuit. I recognised some of the people there, and immediately felt intimidated. I ducked behind the board racks and walked to the back of the shop, avoiding everyone, and almost bumped into a guy who I vaguely recognised from the surf. He was weighing a board in his hands, and he looked surprised when he saw me.

'Whoa! Dude!' he said loudly. 'How's your arm?'

The entire shop looked and I heard Lisa groan. She pushed me past him.

'Good,' I replied. 'Yeah, I'm good.'

I took a steamer off the rack, and stretched into it in the change room. The left sleeve was 5 centimetres too long. The sales guy said, 'Just chop it, man.'

We paid quickly and left. I felt sort of embarrassed.

What am I doing? I'm no pro. If I was a pro, then people would understand. But they must be wondering: Why is he bothering?

I punished myself with that thought. I turned the ignition and soon the car was running, traffic driving past. Lisa put her hand on my shoulder.

'Are you excited?' she asked.

'Nervous,' I said. 'A bit. I'm not sure . . . But, yeah, excited too.'

The next day, at 8.30 a.m., Lisa and I met Damo at Maroubra. It was blowing offshore and the waves were 3 foot high, clean and slightly fat. Lisa walked with us down to the water, a part of her wanting to make sure there was nothing out there. I told myself not to stay out too long, not to put her through that. She cried as I walked towards the water. I could see her whispering to the baby.

I put my legrope on, one-handed.

I'll never get it as tight as I used to. But that's okay.

There have been five shark attacks at Maroubra, and only two of them, back in the 1930s, were fatal. I comforted myself with the knowledge that none of the attacks had occurred in May through October.

Wait until the sun is above the horizon.

The sun was high.

The water came over my feet.

Damo said, 'Just get out the back, paddle around, get the feeling of being out there.'

I wanted to stand up.

He told me to relax. I felt confident with him there. Damo had taken up surfing relatively late in life, in his mid-twenties, but had become good at it quickly. He was good at every sport he tried, and had always been the captain in our rugby teams. Plus he has a knack for saying the right thing.

At the water's edge, Damo said, 'You first.'

I skipped over white water and launched. My board skidded away from me and I face-planted, the ocean consuming me. I came up spluttering foolishly. Damo sailed past and didn't laugh. I pulled my board back to me by its legrope and clambered on. The waves were just big enough to require a decent duck dive, and the first thing I learnt was that I would have to re-learn duck diving. One-handed, I could push the board under the wave, but as the turbulence rolled over me I lost control and came up hanging off the board. It was a struggle to get out the back, and I was so focused on getting out there that I didn't think about what lay beneath.

Out there.

It was beautiful, I remember that.

I sat up. There were a few others out. Damo floated an arm's length away. I could see through the water to the sand.

How do I feel? I thought.

I feel fine, bounced back.

'How do you feel?' asked Damo.

'Just . . . normal.'

I spent thirty minutes paddling in circles trying to catch a wave. I had no paddle power. I was weak and slow and my endurance faded with every wave I tried to catch. Damo said it didn't matter if I didn't get a wave. 'Today is just about being out here, mate.'

I saw Lisa waiting on the shore. I didn't want to paddle in. A bigger wave came and broke on my head. I pushed an almighty duck dive and got hammered. After that, I paddled deeper and waited for a big one. When it came, I ignored everyone that I was going to drop in on and paddled furiously. I kicked hard and felt the wave take me. I stood awkwardly, very late. I just avoided nosediving. The wave closed out and I wobbled and fell. I'd only stood for a few seconds, but, hell, I got up. That was it: if I could do it once I could do it. I paddled back out and floated in the crowd, and felt no fear, and knew I would be a surfer again.

Later, another wave came.

'Go, mate!' shouted Damo.

I flipped and paddled and got up clean and pumped down the line before the wave fattened and died out. I pulled off the back. Damo raised his arm above his head.

I caught a white-water wave in, buggered. I'd been out for an hour: two waves, a hammering, sea water up my nose. I sat on the beach with Lisa and we watched Damo surf. I had wondered about this moment, about how I'd feel after my first surf, but I was too tired to feel much and my mind was spinning:

I need to surf on a bigger board, for a while . . . I could attach a strap to my board for duck diving . . . Be tough getting waves at Bondi, in the crowd . . . I should do push-ups . . . Am I leaning to the right when I get up?

Lisa leaned over.

'Are you okay?'

'Yeah.'

'Happy?'

'Yeah.'

DAY
PLÙS
138

I'd used 20 litres of blood in hospital. It would take me fifty years to repay that amount, so I became an ambassador for the Australian Red Cross Blood Service and together we worked up a promotional event around the 2009 City to Surf that we called 'Running on Blood'. The City to Surf is a 14-kilometre run from Sydney to Bondi Beach, which attracts around 80 000 runners, and our plan was to find a team of at least fifty runners who would ask people to sponsor them by donating blood. We were hoping to raise in excess of a thousand blood donations and to also raise awareness in the community. I promoted the campaign on radio and TV and in newspapers – I got sick of telling the shark story. James McIntosh and I had been in contact and he had built a website for Running on Blood in his evenings after work. He did it because I'd asked him to, but mostly because he's a good person.

From my first days in the ICU, I'd decided I wanted to run in the 2009 City to Surf. One of my life goals was to run the City to Surf in under sixty minutes. I'd run it three times before. The first time, in 2003, I ran the last kilometres down into Bondi while watching the ocean approach through a sea of heads and sunlight and grunts and the sound of hooves on pavement, and I was so happy with myself for making the distance. It took me seventy-five minutes, and I couldn't walk for days afterwards. Each year after that, I'd see pictures of the race in the newspaper and I'd remember the feeling of that downhill run, and feel disappointed that I hadn't run it again.

When I moved in with Lisa in 2007, I ran the City to Surf a second time. I finished in seventy-three minutes, and then sat down on the beach, in sweat-stained exhaustion, drinking blue Gatorade, and watching the surf. After a while I stood, and I felt stiff but I could walk, and someone said to me, 'You don't even look that tired.'

And, looking up the hill at the runners still coming in, I thought, *I can run faster.*

In 2008, I trained hard. I ran 10 kilometres – in the dark, against the headlights – home from work every night. In the race I felt good until the 9-kilometre mark, when my shoelace started slapping my shin. I had to stop for a few frustrating seconds and re-tie the lace while a stream of runners moved around me. I finished in one hour and fifty-five seconds, and I thought about that shoelace mishap. And that's when I decided that I wanted to break the hour.

The City to Surf was a marker in my life. It had come to represent my departure from a life of instability, laziness and self-immolation into a period of being in love, of health, surfing and being alive. In my psyche, the City to Surf was important; I knew that completing a physical goal would bring me confidence. I thought I might be able to beat my old self and beat the hour. I started training hard and focused on that. It took my thoughts away from my arm and my pain.

Through June 2009, I went running every day, and every day I woke up with sore legs, but I enjoyed the 10-kilometre runs home after work. Some evenings I ran 15 kilometres. The solitude of running, the heaving chest, the grittiness of getting somewhere: it hurt, but felt so good.

James McIntosh and I had become friends and he got involved in the Running on Blood campaign. He came with me for my first surf back at Bondi, and Uge Tan from Aquabumps came to take photos that we could release to the media to promote the Running on Blood campaign. James and I scrapped around in small surf, with him in a pair of board shorts, shivering with cold. I floated about, not doing much, while Uge waited patiently to get a shot of me catching a wave. Finally a tiny wave came, a bumpy, fat dribble, and Uge, who was standing in thigh-deep water, projected the camera in my direction as I stood.

It was a great shot, and also an embarrassing one. Uge had captured the gently crumbling green wave, and me surfing, and the clean sky, and the buildings up on Notts Avenue; it was perfectly composed. But, damn, I looked awkward – hair plastered to my face, my stance like I was balancing on a rolling log. I looked like a beginner, and I guess I was, again.

Uge was going to put the photo on the Aquabumps website and write a spiel about Running on Blood. I said, 'With the photos, do you reckon . . .'

'I've got you covered, mate,' he said.

When his daily report came out, Uge included an older photo of me as well, from a few months before the attack, surfing a good wave. So there was a picture of me surfing, and a new picture of me struggling, and the pictures summed up where I had been before, confident in the water, in control, and where I was after, floundering. I was happy with them.

After Uge released his report, the newspapers picked up the story. *The Times* in London called me to do a story. But, most importantly, there were hundreds of blood donations registered. Aquabumps rallied the community, and the local support meant so much to me.

I was excited about Running on Blood, and heartened by my association with the Red Cross, and also beginning to feel like I was back,
physically.

I went to Maroubra on the last day of June. There was one bank
breaking and it was swarmed by surfers. The locals dominated,
catching the sets. I scratched around to the side of the crowd, catching closeout lefts and trying to get in one decent turn (which I hadn't
managed since returning to surfing). After an hour I was tired and
frustrated. I decided to paddle in rather than wait however long it
would take to wrest a wave from the pack.

I started in and was halfway to shore when a set came through.
I sat up and watched a surfer on the first set wave smash two top
turns and run a long arching cutback through a flatter section. He
passed me, stalling his board near the wash, waiting for the wave to
re-form and steepen. I floated over the shoulder. The wave behind
was bigger, and a guy in a blue rash vest with booties on caught
it in one of those inexplicable situations that sometimes happen:
a beginner surfer scoring a set wave from the crowd. When the wave
fattened in the deep section, he fell off. The wave re-formed into
a left-hander. I was in the perfect position. I swung around and
caught it. I took off cleanly. It walled up into a tapered line and
I leaned into a bottom turn, changed my weight and turned the
board, pulling it around into a cutback and bouncing back off the
wash. I turned off the wave as it closed out on the shore. I stumbled
out of the water, onto soft sand.

That was alright! In fact, it was bloody good.

My face warped into a half smile and water dripped off my hair
onto my face.

That was fucken good.

On the shore was a slim guy in a wetsuit, stretching, and he had an impossibly narrow shortboard with sponsorship stickers all over it. My face must have betrayed the song in my head, because he smiled and said, 'Good one?'

'Yeah,' I said.

'It's a good bank, hey?'

'It's a good bank.'

'Have a good one,' he said, launching himself into the water.

I stomped up the beach, living that cutback again and again.

DAY
PLUS
150

The Book of Weeks was finished. I drove Lisa to the hospital ten days overdue. It was time.

The hospital loomed. More hospital time, but now it was the exciting kind, although there was some fear too, especially for Lisa. Walking through the revolving door, with a small bag of clothes, we knew we'd be coming back out with a baby.

The midwife couldn't tell if Lisa was in labour. There was some conjecture.

'It might be good labour.'

Good labour?

It's not encouraging when a new birth word comes along in the maternity ward.

The midwife told her, 'You'll know when you're in labour.'

A contraction or two later, in great pain, Lisa said, 'I tell you, I'm in labour.'

There was no ambivalence on her part. She went through hours of pain, and it was a tough, gritty pain that had her crawling on the floor. She didn't take any drugs and I felt her going inwards to deal with it. It was hard to watch. I felt useless. When Lisa went quiet, screwing up her face, I held her hand – it was all I could do. I swear, my own pain that I'd been going through for months was easier to deal with than those moments of watching Lisa struggle.

It went all night long, and into the next day, and then our baby girl arrived in this world, pink and crying. When I first saw her, I was in shock. Her head was cone-shaped – that threw me. Her eyes were huge and her little mouth was open in a scream that I realise in hindsight was fear, but which looked to me, then, like fury. I didn't realise how scared she was. Our baby needed a lot of love right when she came out, because she had just come into a cold, bright room and was face-to-face with her unshaven, speechless father. I loved her so much.

Wanting to meet my child was one of the things that got me to shore after the shark attack. I owed her for that. They handed me the baby and I cuddled her and spoke to her, and she looked into my face and knew I was her dad.

In the ward room, Lisa recovered and held the baby to her chest. We named her Bronte, and it was then, seeing the love on Lisa's face, that tears came to my eyes. I realised how lucky we were to be a family. There had been a short space of time when I was on the ropes and slipping to the canvas. At the same time as Bronte was finding her way into this world, I was fighting to not leave it. I could have passed out of this reality just before Bronte came into it. I was overjoyed to be able to hold her, to be her father.

When I was a boy, I looked up to my dad. I knew he was right there for me. He knew everything about the world. He didn't question how to be a father, he just was one; he was made that way. And just before Bronte was born, I had compared myself to him and worried about how much less capable I was. I wondered if I was suitable to be a father. And it wasn't until Bronte was born, and I knew her for a little while, that I realised that my father probably hadn't had all the answers. He had likely worried about his children, but my father had wanted me to believe that he was the pillar of my life, and so he made it that way. He did it for me, as a gift.

In reality, I'm sure that he worried irrationally, wondered if he was doing everything right, and snuck into my room at night to watch me sleep – to check my breathing. I'm sure he did that. I'm sure he worried about the harshness of the world, about the hard truth of it at times, and he wanted the same thing for me that I now want for my girl: I want her to believe that I will always be there for her, always. If she believes that now, then it will stay with her, and deep down she will carry it through her life, and it will be there in her toughest moments. Just like my father was for me. I feel like I am here for a reason, and that reason is to look after my family.

DAY
PLUS
178

The first month of a child's life is intense, for everyone. The child discovers a new world, and they are not used to it, and they are *not* always happy about it. Then there is breastfeeding, which can be torture, or bliss, or both at once, and a lot harder than expected either way. Neither Lisa nor I slept well. We knew this would happen, we thought we were ready. But it is only after a month of 11 p.m., 1 a.m., 3 a.m. and 5 a.m. wake-ups every night that you realise there's no such thing as 'ready'. The pressure of that first month found its way into our relationship, and exhaustion magnified relationship fissures into crevasses. My phantom pain flared. Lisa was adjusting to a life with a baby attached to her. All of our previously abundant individual time was gone, evaporated, and there were some tense moments as Lisa and I talked through the storms. So 'Work as a team' became our motto.

And Bronte made it all worth it – her smile, her presence, just watching her.

A month after Bronte's birth was the day of the City to Surf, and I woke up bleary-eyed at 6 a.m. I was alone. Lisa had taken Bronte to her parents' for the night so I could get a full night's sleep before the race. My training had dropped away over the month – tiredness kills motivation to run in the dark. I had thought that one good eight-hour sleep might bounce me back to fitness, but when I rolled out of bed my feet were heavy as I dragged them into the bathroom.

My gabapentin was on the bathroom table. I was down to taking one pill a day. Some days I took none, just to see how I'd do, and though the pain rarely got above a four, I always went back to the gabapentin. If I had a day off it, then I took two the next day. I was worried about letting the latent concentration in my body fade away. That was the real test. I popped a gabapentin into my palm and took it. I could hear my dad downstairs, getting ready.

I was going to do the City to Surf with Dad. He had only a whisper of his knee cartilage left, having worn most of it away in his youth by running 20 miles a day in flat-soled tennis shoes. At forty-five he'd reluctantly had to give running away. The City to Surf was his first race for over twenty years. He'd been training a few times a week, timing himself; he wanted to walk it in under two hours. I could sense his excitement.

We walked to the bus stop, in the early morning, in red Running on Blood t-shirts, surrounded by other runners. At Hyde Park in the city, Dad and I met up with the Running on Blood team, and I saw my French friend Mikael Thomas, who was also running. I gave him a hug. I saw James McIntosh and gave him a hug too. It was a big moment to have them both running. They had saved my life. The Running on Blood team was fifty strong, including my sister, my brother in-law Mike, and Mud, and many other friends and work colleagues, and quite a few people I didn't know who just wanted to be part of it. I made my way to the start, crammed in among shuffling runners. I waited in the sound and blur, and the cool morning air, and the sunlight.

One hour.

I felt good running the first stretch. There is a hill in the middle of the course called 'Heartbreak Hill'; I told myself to smash it. But I got a stitch in my left shoulder halfway up and had to slow down. People streamed past me. At the top, I got another wind. I ran past the roundabout where I'd had to re-tie my shoelace in 2008. With 5 kilometres to go, I was behind time – one minute behind. I knew I could make it up.

My Running on Blood shirt was sodden. I saw Lisa in the crowd waving, and I was hauling in breath so my wave back to her was poor. I got to the high point of the race, knowing it was all down-hill from there, with 3 kilometres to go. I was two minutes behind; I didn't know if I could make up the time, but I let rip on the down-hill, I let my legs fly out beneath me. I ran at full tilt in the last kilometre, but on a slight incline I burnt out. I gave it everything, tasting blood in my throat, and I finished in one hour, one minute and twenty-five seconds – thirty seconds slower than in 2008.

I looked at my stopwatch. It was my second-fastest time. I'd beaten my twenty-year-old self. I'd beaten my thirty-year-old self. It was close to my personal best.

Close enough, I thought.

I'm as good as I was.

I dawdled along the promenade, through a crowd, and watched the surf pumping.

That's it now.

I knew in that moment I was determined to let go of the crutch that was the gabapentin.

A group of people walking in front of me stopped. I stepped around them and walked into the path of two women. They did a double take at the sight of my arm. I smiled at them and they smiled back as we passed.

Am I as good as I was?

I saw a family walking in the throng, and their small boy pointed at me and I heard him say, 'Look at him, Dad.' The dad's eyes rounded, and the mother leaned down to whisper to the boy. The father raised a hand to me, as if to say, *Kids, you know?* I walked on.

It'll be okay . . .

I stood on the grass hill at the south end of Bondi, knowing it was time to make a choice about the gabapentin: to stop was a choice, but to go on taking it was also a choice.

Can I live with some pain?

The crowd streamed by me. I thought that someone in passing would soon ask me what had happened to my arm, because that happened in crowds. Only recently I'd been standing on exactly the same spot when a bearded, shirtless, skinny man, obviously homeless, had approached me. I'd nodded at him and noticed his piercing light eyes, which seemed so much brighter than the rest of him. He had his hand on his heart when he came up close to me.

'Oh, man,' he'd said, looking at my arm. 'Is that from a burn?'

I generally answered this kind of question by saying that I'd had an accident, because I wasn't comfortable with opening up about it all. But there was something about this homeless guy, some note in his voice.

'I was attacked by a shark,' I said.

'Oh, fuck, really? Are you that guy? Whoa. That must have been fucken terrible.'

He'd held out his hand for me to shake, and it was dirty and gnarled. I had a moment of hesitation, but I shook his hand anyway, and his handshake was soft and gentle.

'I'm a caveman,' he told me. 'My cave's got a sofa, a mattress — everything.'

He put his hand on my shoulder.

'I feel for you,' said the caveman. 'But you've just got to get back on the horse, mate.'

Then he'd just walked off, and I'd watched him swagger along.

I had thought about him a lot since then. I wondered about how he thought he had it all, while I thought he had so little. And he'd had such compassion, this caveman, and he really wanted me to get back on the horse – and I'll tell you, honestly, the way that caveman had talked to me, it made me feel loved.

Standing on that same grassy hill at Bondi, sweat still on my brow from the race, and the sounds of the crowd willing runners down the last stretch, I thought, *This is it. Now.*

The shark attack was an aberration, a fluke, in a beautiful life. I would always have pain in my hand; I'd have to accept the pain that stayed. At least I would always be able to feel a remnant of my lost hand, even though every day it was getting harder to remember how it had worked – how it was to live with two hands, what my life had been. I liked being able to wriggle my fingers and clench a fist – even if it was only a phantom. I decided to accept what was left there.

I am as good as I was.

I decided to stop taking the gabapentin.

I left the grass and made my way to the Running on Blood function. All the runners and supporters of Running on Blood turned up. We had raised 700 donations of blood, enough to save 2000 lives.

I rolled into bed that night, tired, and knowing that Bronte would be up in a couple of hours for a feed. I felt unbelievably happy.

I threw out the gabapentin. I never took another pill.

DAY
PLUS
365

By late 2009, I'd found a routine: up early with Bronte, give her breakfast, surf, work. My appointments at the hospital were finished. Often I forgot that I'd lost my hand. Life was full, and comfortable, and demanding. I was content.

One evening Lisa got a message from Grace, the girlfriend of Matt, the young guy with Crohn's disease in the ICU. He had just passed away. It was 7 p.m., Bronte was asleep. I watched Lisa cry. My stomach turned. Matt had fought for a long time. Grace said that, at the end, it was a relief for him to go; he had been through too much. I clenched my jaw. *He was too young.* I remembered his parents and Grace gathered around his bed. The news stayed with me, as did the fragility of life, and the reason people fight so hard for it: for the people they love. That's the beauty in it.

I kept thinking about his death, even in the surf, and I sat up on my board out at Bondi on a messy day and stared at approaching swell, thinking I was lucky. The waves were overhead and it was overcast. A bloke paddled up to me and I tried to recall how I knew him.

'It was me, that night, do you remember?'

Water rocked over my board. That night: *faces looking down on me, wetsuits, dripping hair . . .*

'You were there,' I said.

'I've got a short-arm steamer at home with your blood stained onto it.'

I looked into the water.

'How'd you feel coming back out here?' I asked him.

'Shaky, for a while. But now I'm good.'

'Me, too.'

He smiled.

'I wished I could have done more for you,' he said.

'You did,' I said. 'You did everything.'

A wide set came, lumpy and fast, feathering from way out deep, and we had to scramble to get under it before it cleaned us up. Another wave came behind it, a good wave, and the crowd got into position. Before I lost him in the melee, I yelled out, 'What's your name?' But I missed his reply.

I saw him catch the next wave, and a bigger one came behind it, and two surfers split the peak, nearly running over three others duck diving it. I paddled over the shoulder. I lost him after that. I caught a wave in, and jogged up the beach. It started to rain, and then it rained hard, as I watched the ocean turn mercury-smooth, only textured by lines of swell.

I walked home and let the heavy thrum of the rain drown out my thoughts.

Summer filled 2010's early days with hazy humidity, north-east winds and sloppy wind-swells. On the Australia Day long weekend, Lisa and I went with our friends Pritch and Jen to Shoal Bay. They had a daughter the same age as Bronte, and the two little girls played together happily.

Pritch and I paddled out at One Mile Beach into 2-foot mush, in the middle of the day. The wind was light onshore, and the water warm and silty-dark. A thin crowd did their best on short closeouts. A few minutes in, a team of baitfish leapt out of the water 5 metres away. A minute later, going in the other direction, a school of larger baitfish leapt out of the sea and fell back towards the ocean like raindrops. A fella next to me said, 'I wonder what's chasing them?'

I felt the presence of the juvenile great white. I tried to put it out of mind, but fear was nudging me. I hadn't had shark fear like it since the attack. I forced myself to stay in the water, but I didn't last. I caught a right-hander, did a turn on a crumbly section, and rode it to the beach. I'd been in the water for fifteen minutes. It was the first time I'd ever got out of the water because of shark fear. I stood in the shallows, my board under my arm, and watched other surfers ride the slop. I tried not to berate myself, but it was hard. I told myself that it wasn't forever, it was just for today. I tried to accept that I was different now, more cautious. Pritch came in a while later.

'Pretty crap out there, hey?'

'Yeah,' I said. 'No good.'

Before we drove back to Shoal Bay, Pritch and I checked Birubi Point, and it was good, better than One Mile. Bigger, and the banks looked good. I knew it would be good the next morning when the wind was lighter. Pritch and I watched four surfers on a wedging left, and I could see how murky the water was. Scientists know that Birubi Point appeals to juvenile great white sharks, but they don't know why.

'It'll be good here tomorrow,' said Pritch.

'Yeah.'

We drove home. I didn't tell Lisa about the baitfish.

It was nothing.

We were going to check Birubi the next morning, and if it was good, there would be no denying it – my heart would be in my throat when we paddled out. And, in the morning, Birubi was good: clean, 4 foot, almost pumping. The wind was soft, and the sun was bright.

The sun is above the horizon.

There were tanned families on the beach, kids splashing in the shallows, flags, blankets, umbrellas in the sand. There were some surfers in the water, and out further, on a deep sandbank to the south, were a few of the more intrepid ones; from a distance they looked like ants.

Pritch and I didn't even discuss if it was worth going out. We pulled our boards off the roof and rubbed on sunscreen. I wanted Pritch to go in front, but he was behind me as we waded into the water. I forced myself onto my board and paddled out, close to a group of three surfers. They looked at me, so close to them, when there was so much space nearby.

Lying on my board, I realised that I still had my wedding ring on. I saw it flashing below the water. Its gold shine picked up the sunlight. I'd read that one shark-attack avoidance strategy is to remove all shiny jewellery, because it can be mistaken for fish scales. That had seemed ludicrous to me, but, when you're paranoid, the ludicrous can seem reasonable.

There is so much we don't know about sharks.

I sat up on my board and pulled my feet up onto the deck, and held my hand out of the water, the ring sparkling in the daylight. Pritch caught a wave and rode it the beach. I saw him wade out of the water, gather his legrope, and run back along the shore to the channel near the rocks. I had to go in. I spun around, paddled onto a small lump of swell that actually turned into a good left-hander, and I ended up riding its whitewash in.

I waded onto the sand and pulled my ring off my finger and pushed it into the small Velcro pocket on my legrope. Ahead, Pritch was wading back into the channel. I sprinted along the beach, flung my board onto the sand near the shore and adjusted my legrope.

If he's going back out, then I'm going back out.

I skipped into the water and ducked under waves and paddled like a bastard until I caught up with him. For the next hour or so I shadowed Pritch. I made myself stay in the water.

I'm not getting out until he gets out.

But it was tough staying out there. I felt certain that sharks were under me. I couldn't see them, but I envisaged their fins breaking the water and heading in my direction. Over the previous few months of surfing, in moments when thoughts of sharks came, I'd been comforting myself with the words: *I'll never see it coming anyway.*

Strange words to give comfort, I suppose, but they did. I had no control. Sharks would do what they would do, and there was no point in worrying. I'd chosen to go in the water, no matter the consequences, and once the decision was made, there was no point in worrying. There was no control. If a shark came, I'd never see it, and could never be prepared.

I'll never see it coming.

But the words gave me no comfort that day at Birubi. They had lost their power.

I caught a wave into a no-man's-land about halfway out. I came off in the wash and my board was sucked away. I visualised my legs treading water from below. I yanked at my legrope and the board stalled in the foam. I lessened the tension, then yanked again, and the board came back. I scrambled on top and paddled back out with my heart thumping.

Pritch caught waves to shore, and ran around to the channel, and sometimes I'd follow him, running behind him, and wondering, *Is he really going out again?*

Finally, he looked at me.

'Just catch one more, hey?

'Yep.'

He got the first wave.

I waited on the water, alone, my feet up on my board. After a while, a wave came and I made sure not to make any mistakes on it.

It was one of the worst surfs I'd ever had. I walked up the beach, and for the first time in a long time, I felt a rubber ball of anxiety lodge in my throat.

On the drive back home from Shoal Bay, with Bronte asleep in the back, I told Lisa about it: about the baitfish at One Mile, and my panic at Birubi.

'I've been thinking about it, too,' she said.

'About sharks?'

'About the attack. Everything just feels exactly the same as last year. The weather, your birthday coming up. The anniversary of the attack is only a few weeks away.'

I shook my head. 'I haven't been thinking about it.'

'I have, and it's been bothering me. Maybe it's been getting to you too?'

'I haven't thought about it.'

'But you have this anxiety. That's your old pattern – something going on in you that you are not aware of, and then it comes out as anxiety. Everything feels just the same as last year. The thing is, you will always have to work on this stuff. That's just the way it is, and you'll get good for a while, and then shit will happen, and the old pattern will come back. Just be aware of it.'

On the anniversary of the attack, I took the day off work. It was a beautiful day, and the surf was flat. I walked along Bondi Beach and put my feet into the ocean. Ever since the surf at Birubi, I'd been making myself think about the attack. It was shitty, but I'd been ignoring the feelings associated with the anniversary of the attack and I needed to break that pattern of mine. So I let myself recall the horror of the attack and the paddle in. The fear flooded over me, and passed, and my anxiety started to shift away. This was how I'd learnt to deal with it.

A few days later, I arrived in the Bondi Beach car park at 6.30 a.m. *The sun is above the horizon.*

The south end at Bondi was 4-foot, east-southeast swell with light winds and clear conditions. The banks were holding the swell; it was Bondi on a better day. I strapped my legrope on. My mate Gus, who'd been in the surf with me a year before, dropped down next to me with a massive smile.

'G'day, mate!' he said.

We paddled out together. I felt calm and the waves were excellent. I loved that surf.

Somewhere else the great white turned five years old, and was somewhere near 3 metres long, and, at 300 kilograms, had put on a third of its body weight in the past twelve months. It was still a metre or two off being mature, though. Quite possibly it had moved on from residency at Stockton; the CSIRO hadn't tagged any 3-metre individuals at Stockton. In Australia the white ranges from southern Queensland around the coast to the north of Western Australia. Maybe this great white shark had moved to a new area of the world.

Scientists have noted that some white sharks never make the transition to eating marine mammals; some large specimens have been found with only fish in their stomachs. But I don't reckon this was that kind of a shark; I reckon this one was destined to be a mammal eater, and perhaps it headed off to some seal colony around South or Western Australia. I don't know, of course, but I don't feel like I'll meet it again.

Great whites are portrayed in the media as pathological caricatures, and as malevolent. That's rubbish. It's just that nature is impersonal in many ways, and life needs other life, life needs to eat other life. That is the way of this world. Watch a great white swim, watch it cruise: they are graceful, mighty beasts. I respect them, and fear them; I don't want them near me, but they are not sadistic. I hope we learn more about them – they've been the subject of considerable research over the last twenty years, but the biology and behaviour of great whites are still mysteries.

I don't like that marine animals are trapped in shark nets. I'm not even convinced the nets protect us, and these animals may be suffocated for nothing. The thought of them fighting, dying, in a net upsets me. I hope this great white shark doesn't end up like that. This one might live for another fifty-five years; I really hope it does.

DAY
PLUS

I am going home. I walk along city streets and it is warm and humid and my shirt sticks to my back. At a traffic light I see my reflection race by in a bus window, and because I'm wearing my suit, and my bionic hand, I look like the man I once was: a man with two hands. But he was never as full up with life as I am now. He lived in his head, unaware of the forces that drove him into paranoia. I am not that. I have found who I am, and I am content. Perhaps I'm not as physically able as the man I was, but I am a more capable man than him and I am glad that he's gone.

Here is one true thing: I am one-handed, but it is not that important.

My daughter knows that I am different.

'Daddy only got *one* arm,' she says.

'One hand,' I say.

Her small nose crinkles.

'Bit sad?'

She means: is my arm sad, and am I in pain.

'No, darling, I'm okay.'

She smiles and I tickle her chin.

'Silly daddy,' she says.

I am not lying when I tell my daughter that I'm okay, but my arm *is* a bit sad. I live with an inconvenient pain. I don't expect that it will ever go away entirely. This is okay. It is not that important.

My train arrives at Bondi Junction and I walk into the sun, to the car park. I open my car door and feel the heat come out that has been stuck inside it all day. Traffic lights go green and red and stay red for a long time. I slide down my seat and tap the brake pedal. Lisa and Bronte are waiting for me.

At the beach I see our pram and a yellow bucket and a spade leaning on the sand. I see my wife and child walking along the shore. They turn and giggle, and I know that their lives are so much more precious than mine. I hold Lisa and I pick up Bronte at the water's edge, my feet sinking in the sand. I carry Bronte into the sea, with her grabbing me up high around my neck. The water is calm and warm and Lisa dives in and pops up near us, and Bronte laughs. Chest deep, I turn my back to the horizon, and let whatever's out there be, as a tiny swell wraps gently around my back.

All the time I have, I'll remember these moments of us together. And I'm glad there is no surf, that just for today there is no distraction, because I want this family time. This is what's important. This is why I paddled in.

ACKNOWLEDGEMENTS

I am grateful to Mikael, Seb, James, Connor, Mick, Gus and Shahbaz for sharing their account of events on 12 February. To all of them, and all the other people on the beach that night, and the paramedics and staff from St Vincent's and Prince of Wales hospitals – thank you.

Rick, Sarah and Tim, thanks for your support through the years, and for taking me to Peats Ridge in 2006.

To A&A and the Slades, thanks for your encouragement, and all the Friday nights.

I'd like to thank my editor, Cate Blake, for backing this project and for her support, understanding and great advice.

To my parents, Jan and Ric, thanks for being there always, and especially when I have needed you most, and for your reviews of early drafts.

To my little Bronte, you light up my every day.

To Lisa, who endured the reading of many early drafts and also various histrionics of mine, and who made this book possible, and whose chutzpah helped me get it published – thank you. This book is for you.